For permission requests, contact:
lunahopethomsen@gmail.com

ISBN: 9788797528808
001 edition, 2025

Author's Note

This book wasn't edited by a fancy publishing house. It was edited by coffee, crying, and the occasional typo I still haven't found.
I didn't want this story to feel polished or distant, because that's not how it was lived. It was raw. Messy. Full of stops, with rewrites, and emotional U-turns.
So I kept it that way on purpose. Not because I'm lazy. Not because I'm broke. (Okay, sometimes that too.)
But mostly because I wanted you to feel like you were sitting across from me, not reading from a pedestal.

Some publishers were interested, but they wanted *pieces* of the story.
Just the drama, or just the healing, or just the parts that made people cry in public.
But I couldn't cut it up like that. This is all of it. And I wanted to tell it **my way** — not as a product, but as a person.

So this book is what happened when I stopped waiting for permission and started writing anyway.

If you spot a typo, just pretend it's a tear stain.

Thank you for reading, and for coming this close.
I hope you feel seen here, the way I wish I had, when I lived these pages.

If it hurts, it means it mattered. That's all I ever hoped for.

CONTENTS

PROLOGUE

I found Mom's scarf hanging on the hallway door. The brown one with the scratchy edges. She used to wear it when she wanted to look nice, like when people came over. I never liked how it smelled; like flowers that aren't real. But today I put it around my neck anyway. I don't know exactly why.

I sat on my bed, looked at the mirror on my closet and tried to make a serious face. I made my lips tight and didn't blink much. Like in the movies, when someone important has something important to do. I wanted to look like I had a big plan, even though I just felt scared.

My hands were shaking a little, but I told them to stop. I told them we were just playing. Just pretending.

My head started to feel floaty, like when I spin too fast and the room takes a second to catch up. My stomach turned cold. Like the fear started in my bones and was working its way up. Even my skin felt scared, like it didn't want to be touched by air. I remember thinking: *Maybe if I do this right, no one will ever yell at me, or beat me ever again.*
I even made a deal in my head: If I stay still enough, if I don't cry, maybe an angel will come. Maybe someone will notice. Maybe I'll wake up and today will be different. I always left that maybe hanging, like a string tied to a balloon I never got to hold. I could almost hear the silence I wanted, like a soft blanket wrapping around me. If I did it right, maybe the bad sounds would stop. Everything got slower, quieter. It was like the whole world was holding its breath with me. But then the scary feeling came back, louder.

Then I got really scared. I couldn't feel the air going in or out right, and it felt like my body didn't know what to do. I just wanted someone to help me. I wanted someone to grab me tight and tell me it was going to be okay. I didn't know what was happening, not really. I just knew I needed my mom, so I loosened the scarf, and that's when I felt it, my neck hurt. Not a lot, but enough to know I had done something real. Something wrong. I didn't want it to be real. I wanted my mom. I let the scarf slip off like a mistake I couldn't explain, and I ran to her. She was doing the dishes. I waited for her to look at me, but she didn't. Her hands kept moving, splashing water like the mess inside me.

I stood there quiet for a second, then I looked at the floor and whispered, "Ana hawelt amoot." I said it in Arabic, because I didn't know how to say that other word. The one that sounded serious. I didn't think she'd understand it anyway.

She looked at me like I had done something wrong. Like I ruined her day. Her face got tight and angry.

"Next time," she said, "use a rope."

Then she looked away, like I wasn't even there.

I went back to my room and didn't say anything else. It's dark in my room. Really dark. But that darkness wasn't just in the room; it was starting to live inside me, too. I didn't have words for it yet, but it was a kind of sadness that didn't go away with morning. I don't like the dark, but I don't turn on the light. I just stay under the blanket, pretending I'm invisible.

Then I hear it again.

Her scream cuts through the walls.
Sharp.
Sudden.
Like someone ripped the night open.

I pressed my hands over my ears, but it was inside my head too, like an alarm that wouldn't stop.
"Again!" I think and then freeze. My whole body goes still. I feel it in my chest, like my heart is jumping around, scared. I wanted to run, but my legs weren't legs anymore, they were part of the bed, part of the fear. I squeezed my eyes shut and curl up tight in my messy bed. I hold Cindy, my soft doll, tight against my chest. I try to make myself small, like the fear won't find me if I don't move.

From somewhere in the house, I hear his voice.
"I saved you from your poor and miserable life! I brought you here! Remember that!"
That's my dad. He says that a lot, like he did us all a favour by being here. Like we should say thank you when he's mean.

Then her voice comes back, sharper than ever. She's in the kitchen. "You're old, you son of a bitch! Nobody wants you! I'm only still here for the kids!" shouting at my dad.

I wished the yelling could turn into whispers, soft and kind.

Their voices bang against the walls like angry fists.
I can't see them, but I know where they are in the house. I know all the spots where yelling happens. It's like the house has bruises, too.

I push my blanket over my ears, but I can still hear everything. Their fighting is like a song that never ends. A bad song with the same words over and over. I squeeze my eyes shut until the inside of my head goes quiet. But the silence was just the space between the next shouts.

Then,
Knock Knock.

Not loud. Soft. That means it's my little brothers.
Mom never knocks. She kicks the door open.

I pull the blanket off and get out of bed. They didn't say anything. They just climbed in next to me, like we were making a secret safe place. I open the door, and there they are. Both. Their faces look scared. I think mine does too.

I let them in. They crawl into my bed without saying anything, and I hug them both. I try to make my arms strong, like a shield, even if I feel weak inside. I don't want them to know I'm scared too. "Shh," I whispered. "I'm here." Even if I didn't feel it.

Then I yell, as loud as I can without crying,
"Mom, please! It's late! The neighbours are sleeping!"

But she doesn't stop. I hear her sobbing.
Then I hear it, slaps. I know that sound.
She's hitting herself again.
She's hitting herself again.
Slap. Slap.
Like she's trying to erase her face.

Then silence. But not really silence. That's the sound of her yanking her hair. I know the pattern now.

Slap.
Pull.
Slap.
Pull.
It's like a heartbeat.

Boom, slap.
Boom, pull.

My heart tries to follow the sounds, like it's confused.

Dad says, like he's spitting, "She's crazy. What have I gotten myself into? She is *crazy!*"

And while Mama is really upset, she keeps hurting herself and pulls at her hair so hard I think it might come out, and she slaps her own face also, over and over, each slap, a secret debt she was repaying. I wanted to catch the pain and hold it so it wouldn't hurt her anymore. And while she does it, she screams things, awful things. That she's going to walk into the sea and keep walking until the water takes her. That she'll go up to the fourth floor and jump. That she'll wait for a truck and throw herself in front of it. But I can't forget it. I can't stop thinking about what she said.

So now, when she gets ready to go out, unless it's for work, or taking the trash, or buying food, I watch her. I pay attention to how her face looks, to the way she moves. I try to guess if it's one of those days.

And when she leaves, I sneak to the window and peek through the curtain to make sure she goes to the car.
I watch to see that she drives off. I need to be sure she didn't just walk away to go do one of the things she screamed about.

It feels like I'm the only one checking if she's still going to be alive. Like it's my job now. Even if I don't really know how.

When Mama screams about ending her life, I'd press my ear to the door and whisper, 'Please don't go, Mama. Please.' Sometimes I think I whispered it so quietly, even God couldn't hear me. But after a while, it didn't sound strange anymore. It was scary, yes, but also kind of normal. Like part of how things worked in our house. If things got too hard, if the pain got too loud, then you talked about not wanting to be alive anymore. She said those things like they were just facts. Like walking into the sea and not stopping was a real option. Like jumping from the fourth floor could be a kind of silence. So, when she goes to her room, I press my ear to the door. Just for a second. I don't hear crying. I don't hear anything. Sometimes nothing is scarier than yelling. Nothing means I don't know what comes next.

And I didn't know it then, not really, but hearing that over and over did something to me.

It made it seem like maybe that's what people do when they hurt too much. I noticed how often people disappeared emotionally before they ever disappeared physically. Like my mom, who would vanish into silence or her rage. That maybe pain is something you escape by leaving for good. That maybe if you feel like you can't breathe inside your life anymore, then disappearing becomes a way to survive it.

I didn't understand all of that yet. But the ideas were already sitting quietly inside me, growing roots.
One day, they would come back. One day, I would hear myself thinking them too. Not because I wanted to, but

because they had always been there, whispered like lullabies by the person who should have been teaching me how to stay.

Those horrible things, she's not saying them to me. She's not even really looking at me. It's like she's stuck inside her own storm and I'm just standing there, sometimes watching it ripping her apart. I don't know what to do. My feet freeze. My heart thumps so hard it hurts. I don't know if I'm supposed to stop her or hide or pretend, I can't hear her. And what makes it even scarier is that after all that, after all the screaming and pulling and hitting, sometimes she just stops. Like nothing happened. Like she didn't just say all those scary things. She might go quiet, clean something, make tea.

But I can't go quiet. My body is still shaking. I wanted to peel my skin off and hang it on the wall, like maybe it would stop vibrating if I wasn't wearing it. My ears are still ringing. And I never know when it will start all over again.

So, I stay small. Careful.
Disappear.
Maybe the storm won't see me next time.

But tonight, she's screaming again. Hurting.
I hold my brothers tighter.
I try not to shake.
I want to be the grown-up. I want to be the one who says everything will be okay. But all I can do is keep holding them, and hope the night goes quiet again, so I can accompany them to their rooms when all is quiet.

After they keep yelling back and forth for a long time, it finally stops. I think Mom went back to the dishes again.

But we have a dishwasher. Oh, I forgot, water costs a lot. All that time she spends doing dishes... she could be playing with us instead. But maybe I don't want her to play with us. I don't think I can ever do anything to make her happy. The only time she looks happy is when she's crying, and I hug her and make her feel better.

Then she seems a little less sad. Or when she hits me with my father's belt, the brown one, it hurts a lot. But I prefer the brown one, because the black one is bigger, like a snake. The more I cry, the louder I cry, the happier she seems. But then she shouts, "Shut up! Shut your mouth! Or I'll break your mouth!"

So, what am I supposed to do? How can I make her be nice to me and my brothers? What am I doing wrong? If I cry, scream, am silent, talk back, all I do is wrong.
Maybe I'm not doing anything wrong... Maybe I *am* the wrong thing. Like the mistake she didn't mean to make but now can't throw away. Maybe I'm the reason she cries. Maybe just being alive is wrong, that's why she's so sad all the time.
And my brothers... She can hit me if she wants. But if she hits my brothers, I'll do whatever I have to make her stop. I want them to be safe, even if that means I get hurt instead.
I can handle it. I just can't stand to see them hurt.

I became their bedtime soldier, guarding them from monsters that weren't under the bed but already in the house. I was nine years old with a battlefield in my chest and no helmet. But I swore, if she came for them, she'd have to go through me first. Even if it meant I wouldn't make it.

Then I hear footsteps outside my door. My heart stops. I hold my breath, hoping it's not her. But I know that sound... it's her steps, loud and heavy, like trouble coming.

I want the noise to stop. I want her to go away.

The door opens slowly. She stands there, her hair, messy and her face all red and tired, but her voice is calm when she says, "Why aren't you sleeping? It's late. You have school tomorrow."

I try to say something, but the words get stuck.
"We can't sleep when you're screaming. Why did you hit yourself? Does it hurt? I don't want my brothers to hear—" She calmly cuts me off, "Then don't sleep. I don't care." She slams the door, goes back to the kitchen. I'm left shocked and confused, so I bring my brothers to their rooms.

When I go back to my bed, I don't know what's going on in my brothers' rooms. Their feelings are too big for me to understand. The house feels heavy and sad.

I wish I could help them, but I don't know how.
I feel like I'm failing.
I wish this was a one-time thing, but it's not.
This is what life is like for me, every single day and night.

I speak French. She speaks Arabic.
But pain? It needs no translation.
So, we yell. We hide.
We stay alone.
We don't know how to say what's hurting inside us.

And sometimes, I try to make her see how sad I am by hurting myself, hoping she'll feel it too.
See it, see *me*.

My father doesn't say anything. He just lies on the couch. The TV is on, talking in Arabic, louder than his quiet. The noise from the TV seems to make Mom even angrier. And if things get too much for him, he runs away from home. He goes to a bar and comes back late at night when everyone is sleeping.

Sometimes, if Mom hears him come back late, she starts screaming and it wakes us up, we become startled. Then it's hard to fall back asleep.
When I can't sleep, and she is screaming, my mind is busy, thinking about my brothers, school, about how I'll get through tomorrow, and most of all, about home. Home is the hardest part. I must be strong all day just to make it there, to face what's waiting for me.

Then the night comes again, and Mom's yelling rips me out of sleep. The sound fills the room, and I feel like I can't breathe. I want to fall asleep, and I hope when I finally can, I never wake up again. Maybe if I believe it strong enough, it will happen.

I'm just a kid. I don't really get why any of this is happening. It all feels too big inside me. Every sound makes me jump; a door slamming down the hall, a car honking outside, even the fridge buzzing like it's angry too.

I think, therefore I am.

It's one of the most famous declarations in philosophy. A brutal certainty. A cornerstone of selfhood. But what if the thoughts lie? What if, from the beginning, your mind was shaped not by wonder or love, but by survival, trained to flinch before it could flourish?

I grew up being told by my parents, *shown*, that *I was not*. Not enough. Not wanted. Not worth it. Not real in the ways that mattered. And so, I learned to vanish in plain sight, to become smaller than my body, quieter than my screams, more pleasing than my truth.

I remember once standing in the hallway for ten minutes, hoping my mom would notice the bruise blooming on my arm. She walked right past me, talking to herself about the problems she had to deal with at work. I don't think she saw me at all.

If Descartes was right; if I think, therefore I am, then no wonder I felt like a ghost. My thoughts had never been mine alone, they were inherited from fear, stitched together from other people's violence and silence.
Then what does it mean to only think you are unworthy?
Does that make unworthiness your identity?
Does it make the damage your essence?
Because now, in adulthood, the echo of those messages still lives in me. And some days, I don't just hear them, I believe them. I live them. And if that belief defines me, am I then who I was always meant to be? Or am I simply the consequence of a life unloved? Who might I have been, if I had been nurtured? If someone had looked me in the eyes and said,
"You matter. You are safe. You are good."

I wonder: What would I think then? And if I thought differently...
Who might I be?

This story is not the end of me. It's the digging up. The dusting off. The slow and aching reconstruction of a self that never got to fully arrive.

That day, I untied the scarf. I didn't know it yet, but it was the first thread. Years later, I'd start pulling at all of them; every lie, every bruise I pretended wasn't there. And somewhere beneath the knots and silence, I'd find a girl who never got to arrive.

This story is how I brought her home.

PART 1

SHATTERED, NOT BROKEN

Memories of those early years are reduced in a fog, like a protective zone my mind created to shield me from horrors too deep to face. Yet, no shield is perfect. Flashbacks surge unexpectedly, echoes from a past where love was tangled with pain, where safety was a stranger, and home felt more like a battleground.
The person meant to nurture me, the one who should have been my refuge, became the architect of my pain.
I remember her voice trembling with rage as she threw open my bedroom door, her silhouette framed by the hallway light, a belt in her hand. 'You think you can lie to me?' she'd scream, and I'd forget how to breathe.

And in all of this, my father's silence was no less a wound, a quiet and painful absence that deepened the darkness.

Her hands were made for comfort but trained for war. They could stroke your hair and throw a chair, all in the same breath. hen words failed to express my pain, she inflicted marks — some on my skin, others stitched into my memory — that no child should ever learn to flinch for, but I remember hugging her tightly when she was calm, my cheek pressed to her chest, trying to memorize the rhythm of peace. But I also remember the same arms flinging a laundry basket at me the next morning.

Every turn of the doorknob was a roulette wheel. I never knew if it would be dinner or discipline, or both, depending on the seasoning.
Love or violence.
No in-between.

Amid this chaos, I learned a terrible lesson: tears brought more pain, so I buried them deep inside. "Asking for help," I was warned, would invite strangers to tear us apart, take us away from our home.
The fear of being broken apart by outsiders forced us to endure the unbearable, binding us together with invisible chains of fear and confusion. Yet, despite the storm, we were not broken.
Perhaps shattered, fragmented, but never broken. Because I found pieces of myself in quiet acts: writing in a journal I hid behind the radiator in my room, brushing my sister's hair while our mother sobbed in the next room. Those moments didn't fix anything, but they kept me from dissolving. Because to be broken implies a wholeness once existed, yet maybe, for us, those cracks were the shape of our truth from the start.

My little sister, though, was the first real joy of my life. I had always dreamed of having a sister; someone to play with, someone who might just understand me.
So, when Mom picked me up from school one day and casually announced, "I'm pregnant, with a girl. Do you want a little sister?" it felt like she was putting the decision on me, like the fate of this unborn child was in my hands. It was not a question of whether I wanted her. Of course, I did, she knew that. But I could not help but feel like I was being asked to decide her existence, as if *I* were the one who would give her the green light to be born.

So, I jumped for joy, thrilled by the idea of a sister. But what did I know about decisions like that at the time? All I knew was that I'd have someone to take care of, someone who might need me.

But I don't remember her early years, nothing from her birth to when she turned six. It's like she was never there until she was old enough for me to protect her. And that's the part I remember: the moments when I had to keep her safe, even when I wasn't sure how to keep myself safe.
The sadness in this? I don't have memories of being her sister; I only remember auditioning for the role of a mother with stage fright.
I only remember the responsibility, the quiet understanding that I had to be there for her in the ways I couldn't be for myself.
I don't recall playing with her or laughing with her when she was a toddler. What I remember is the heavy sense of being her protector, a role I took on without question. She became my priority from the moment she was born, I know that.
And I wasn't prepared for it.
In that way, I became her mother, in both small and big ways.
I might not remember all those moments, but I know I was the one who held her together, even when I couldn't hold myself together.

–

Every night, the dinner table became a battlefield. Peace

was a fleeting dream, found only when I skipped meals and retreated to my room — a small fortress of solitude where I could momentarily breathe. But even then, peace was fragile. The watchful eyes of suspicion lurked, her tendency to silently observe me through the window of my room to make sure that I am not doing something I am not supposed to do, her gaze a silent accusation that I could never fully escape.

So, in my quiet rebellion, I found that peace in the digital world, clutching my phone or computer as lifelines.

It was a glowing exit sign from my reality. Nobody cried behind notifications. My screen was a glittering lie, but at least it didn't yell. If you're puzzled by how someone repeatedly betrayed can still trust openly, it's because each new connection offered the possibility of rewriting an old script.

Every friend, every acquaintance was a silent question: Can this be different? Trauma didn't steal my hope entirely; it just taught me to wear it like armour, always heavy, always there, and almost always misplaced.

But armour can't stop memories.

They don't respect defences or polite boundaries. They don't knock. They kick the door in with steel-toed boots, wipe their feet on my boundaries, and sit down like they pay rent.

It's important to understand this: the things we go through; those trials, wounds, and scars, are not who we are. Our experiences shape us, yes, but they do not define us.

It's not how we cope that defines us; it's what we grow despite. Some flowers claw their way through concrete and still bloom crooked. And in some cases, in my case, it was impossible without outside help.

What we endure is only *part* of our story.

What we become in the face of adversity, the kindness

we show ourselves and others, the strength to continue, these are the threads that weave our identity. To cope is to survive moment to moment, but to become is to transform, to transcend the pain and make meaning from it.

As Maya Angelou (who I deeply admire) famously said, "I can be changed by what happens to me. But I refuse to be reduced by it." And this refusal, that fierce, quiet defiance, is where our power lies. Not in pretending the pain never existed, but in choosing how it shapes us, how we carry it forward, and how we use it to fuel growth and empathy. I will write more about the ways I coped, including the ugly parts. The parts that looked like strength but were just high-functioning despair.
Some of them healthy. Some of them holy. Some of them a little bit horrifying. Sometimes surviving but other times destroying myself; about the paths that led to healing, the small and big lights that pulled me from the darkness; and about the battles I continue to face each day.

This is not just a story of pain, but a story of resilience, transformation, and hope. Because healing is not a destination, it is not comfortable, but a journey; one I walk with honesty, courage, and an open heart. I share this story not to dwell in sorrow, but to honour resilience, mine and that of every person who has faced the unthinkable and chosen to keep living, keep hoping, or even those who don't know how, but try to.
To anyone reading this and whispering, "me too", you're not alone, and you're not too much.
Just too unseen.

Because surviving is its own kind of victory. But becoming — despite it all — is the kind of miracle you don't find in churches.

Only in the mirror.

–

Within the fabric of my cultural upbringing, I gradually came to understand a profound truth: my mother was not simply difficult or unpredictable, she was unwell, burdened by untreated mental health struggles that cried out for urgent care. Yet in a society where mental illness is cloaked in stigma, often equated with insanity, even speaking the word "psychologist" was a challenge that felt like walking a tightrope.
Time and again, I gathered the courage to suggest she seek help, only to be met with the same cold dismissal: "I am not crazy."

The heavy weight of cultural expectations trapped her in denial, where admitting to pain or struggle meant risking a label so shameful and isolating it was nearly unbearable. What will the family think? What will the neighbour's gossip about? People's opinions have always mattered in a way that I never understood.
She wore my skin tone like a passport; pale enough for approval and fair enough to win silent beauty contests no one claimed to judge but everyone noticed.
But pride is complicated. In her eyes, beauty was a delicate balance, measured in shades of whiteness and scales of kilograms. If I gained weight, meals subtly shrank; if I lost too much, portions grew again.
My body, her careful masterpiece, constantly sculpted, never mine. She never said it outright, but the skinnier I got, the safer I seemed. Like disappearing was the only way to be seen. If I couldn't please her with words or

achievements, maybe I could please her with bones. All subconscious math. This wasn't something I could confront her about, then again, I couldn't confront her about the weather, dinner, or the fact that she'd left her keys in the fridge again. Accountability wasn't her strong suit. Denial, on the other hand, she wore like Chanel. But victimhood was her signature dish: served cold, overcooked with self-pity, and garnished with passive aggression.

A typical conversation unfolded like bad improv theatre: She'd return from work and immediately collapse into complaint: "I haven't eaten, haven't sat once today, I worked from eight to half past four, even did dishes at the canteen."
I'd carefully interject, trying logic on for size: "Mama, if you exhaust all your energy there, what's left for home? You still have all this physical labour waiting, and you can't even sleep..."
But her gaze would slide off me, glassy-eyed, dissociating into a private reverie about martyrdom.
A beat would pass, then she'd proudly announce, as if presenting a medal: "My boss told me I'm brave today. Said I always give my all."

My heart would tighten, anger and sadness wrestling silently inside my ribcage. Anger, because my words evaporated like steam before they could touch her. Sadness, because her suffering, sleeplessness, and pallid face meant less to her than praise from a figure of authority. I'd try again, softly: "Mama, did you even hear what I—"
But she'd cut me off, shifting gears at breakneck speed. "The pharmacist today was so kind, gave me medicine on credit. 'See? Everyone loves me,'" she'd beam, triumphant, as though universal affection justified every skipped meal and sleepless night.

And there I stood, silent, stunned into helplessness, anger, disbelief. My throat choked with words too big to escape: How do you argue with someone building their altar out of suffering, one skipped meal and unpaid pharmacy bill at a time?
How do you convince someone that love shouldn't feel like starvation?

When doctors prescribed antidepressants, offering a glimpse of hope through medicine, she refused to take them, unwilling to concede that there was anything wrong with her.
I kept nudging: "Mama, the pills could help."
She scoffed, flicking the box into the bin. "I'm not turning into a zombie. A tablet can't clean up my mess."
"How do you know," I muttered, "when you never swallow even one?"
She slammed the cupboard so hard it sounded like punctuation. "Because I just know. Now get out of my face." I glanced into the trash at the pills; tiny hopeful soldiers dishonorably discharged before basic training even began.

In her mind, problems required solutions, and since there was no "problem," there was no need for help. The walls around her mind grew thicker, shutting out the very care she desperately needed.
This invisible cage of cultural norms wrapped her pain in bubble wrap and told her to smile through it. I guess no one wants to see the cracks in a good mother.
The very remedies that could bring relief were taboo and stifled by deeply ingrained beliefs that held us captive.

In this complicated dance between culture and mental health, I found myself fighting not just against my mother's resistance, but against a system that

perpetuated silence and misunderstanding.
Through it all, my heart was torn, empathy intertwined with fury. I longed to break these chains, to guide her toward the healing she deserved on the most human level. Yet I knew that true change would require a seismic shift; a cultural awakening that mental illness is not madness, but a human experience needing compassion and support.
As I walked my own path toward understanding, I vowed to challenge the status quo, to tear down the walls of silence around mental health in my culture, in my family.

–

At the age of sixteen, I found the courage to capture the reality of our lives, a house consumed by neglect and anger. Armed with a trembling hand and a flickering hope, I recorded it all — the hoard, the walls marred by bugs and gaping holes, remnants of my youngest brother's uncontrollable rage.
Every detail meticulously documented, a silent cry for help. And then, with the weight of my fears bearing down upon me, I went on the internet, seeking contact with a social worker that Google suggested to me.
In the call that followed, I pleaded with her, my voice trembling with an urgency born from desperation.
"Please don't tell it was me," I begged, my heart hammering, my voice breaking like I'd just confessed to arson, not honesty. But fate, like every adult in my life, completely ignored the assignment.
The social worker, bound by her professional duty, chose a different path. A formal letter arrived, its words cold and calculated, striking fear into my mother's trembling heart. It was an invitation to her office, extended to the

entire family: my father, my mother, my siblings, and myself.

My mother's mind raced, consumed by a maddening curiosity. Who had dared to report her? I offered a carefully crafted lie, blaming a neighbor with whom she had quarrels. She believed me, her fury stoked to an inferno. She kept ruminating out loud (very loud) about this "neighbor" who had reported her, every day leading up to the meeting.

When the appointed day arrived for our troubled family. Around the round table, a psychologist and a social worker were present. The air was heavy with tension. And then, like a twisted conductor, the social worker exposed her damning evidence; the very pictures and videos I had collected.
It was a spectacle of pain and dysfunction, a grotesque theater of our lives laid bare.
In my mother's eyes, I saw the determination that spelled my downfall. I turned to my siblings, but they hesitated, their voices silenced by fear and the twisted loyalty bred within our suffering. And so, I crumbled under the weight of their betrayal, tears falling down my face.

The social worker's interrogation continues. And I, fueled by fear and sorrow, refused to surrender. I feel betrayed and unable to comprehend whether she understands what situation she is leaving me with.
I told the truth; each word was a small rebellion.
The truth didn't save me. But it set something on fire. And when the smoke filled the room, at least I knew where the exits were.
In our home, honesty wasn't brave; it was dangerous. So, the moment my voice rose above the hush, my mother's eyes didn't flinch. Just narrowed, like a sniper choosing

where to aim; not with surprise, but with a quiet, calculated promise: *There will be consequences. Ones you'll have trouble forgetting.*

With the meeting concluded, the social worker offered me a promise, a whisper of hope buried under bureaucratic formalities. "Thank you," she uttered, her words ringing hollow. "We will process your case with our educator and psychologist. We will get back to you."
Spoiler: they never did. But my mother did. Her version of follow-up came with teeth.
And so, I was sent back to the lion's den, the car ride home shrouded in an oppressive silence.
As my mother's fury erupted once again, and with the car window open, her screams echoed through the street like sirens no one wanted to answer. At every red light, strangers turned to stare like we were a roadside accident that just kept happening, but inside a moving car. Their expressions were a mix of concern and revulsion, eyes silently voicing the same unspoken warning: *Don't get too close. Whatever this is... it's not safe.* But she dwelled in chaos, stuck in her distorted perception of righteousness.
"Let them hear," she spat, her voice a piercing dagger.
"Let the world hear what a little traitor you are!" she shrieked. “The neighbor? Really? You pig. You ungrateful pig.”
Between this and the belt beatings, I was basically livestock with opinions.

And then, in a moment that would forever be carved into me, the car became a theater of violence. The blows rained down upon me, each strike leaving a wound upon my flesh and soul. Even my siblings backed her up by screaming at me, their voices betraying the very blood that bound us. One of them wouldn't meet my eyes. The other crossed his arms like a mini soldier, nodding along with every word she spat. And I stood there, watching

them choose survival over truth, the way I had too many times before.
I couldn't blame them. We were all trying to keep our heads above water, we just stopped caring who we pushed under.
But there were lighter moments too; hidden laughter in forts, where being a tomboy bought me entrance into their club. We built shacks from broken wood and rusty nails, serious faces plotting escape routes, just in case Mom came sprinting out, belt in hand.
It wasn't innocence, more like a ceasefire. But we built it ourselves.

In the aftermath of that fateful day, the bruises on my skin would fade, but those etched upon my spirit would remain. From that day, I knew that the price I had paid was but a taste of the agony that awaited me on this path of survival.

If my own family turned a blind eye to my pain, I clung to the hope that the social system, with its promises of protection, would embrace me in its comforting grasp. But as I reached out, my fingers trembling with anticipation, I found only emptiness.
No one picked me. Not family. Not God. Not even the system designed for kids like me.
Not my family, bound by their own demons and blind to the depths of my despair.
Not society, suffocating under the weight of its own indifference, and too busy sorting paperwork to notice bleeding children.
Not my friends, who danced upon the surface of shallow connections, unaware of my desperation.
Even death ghosted me. Not even its cold arms opened when I begged.
And with the haunting question that lingered within me:
What was wrong with me?

I searched for answers, my heart filled with self-doubt and yearning.
Was I just born with the kind of face people forget to worry about?
Did I carry some invisible mark, branding me unworthy of love or compassion?
Was my hunger for help just a delusion, some desperate, imagined need I kept pushing for, until it made me a burden in the eyes of those I reached for?
The shadows of self-blame danced around me, their whispers taunting me with the notion that I was fundamentally flawed. I questioned the very essence of my being, seeking answers in the corners of my tired soul. But each turn revealed only more uncertainty and the fear that perhaps I was destined to wander this lonely path alone.

Yet somewhere in the static, a flicker of "fuck this" caught fire, yes. Not confidence, but refusal.
Refusal to accept that this, this cruelty, this silence, this exile, was all I was worth. It was not a roar, not yet. Just a whisper: *this isn't right*.

In the face of rejection and abandonment, I didn't rise, I clenched.
I held on.
I didn't know to whom or what, but something in me gripped tight to the idea that I could become more than what they made me feel. Safety had been a myth I read about in books and watched in movies. But even then, some part of me began to believe that if I didn't belong *there*, then I could belong *somewhere* — even if I had to build it from scratch.

I'm not there yet. I'm still searching. Still trying to define "home" when all I learned was how to dodge flying objects and say thank you for leftovers.

But I'm trying.

Trying to find a place in the world. Trying to feel like I deserve to be in it.

Trying to find home. Not the one I came from,
the one I'll choose, or the one that'll choose me.

But sometimes, these questions arise: Who dares believe they're worthy of soft things like love, safety, or consistency? What kind of lunatic bets on that kind of magic twice?
Because if I believe in those things, I open the door to hunger. To betrayal. To the brutal kind of disappointment that takes years to scrape off your ribs.
So, no. I'd rather stay empty than be full of borrowed promises that expire the second I get attached.
I would rather be empty by choice, than full of hope I didn't ask for.
It's not that I don't want love. It's that I don't want to bleed for it anymore.

And yet... somewhere deep inside, the hunger remains.
Hope still rattles its chains.
I don't feed it. But I still hear it scratching.

Quiet. Not gone.

Just caged, for now.

–

You might be asking yourself why I didn't seek professional help earlier, why therapy wasn't my first

option rather than my last resort.
The truth? Seeking help felt like admitting that I was irreparable, beyond divine intervention.
Therapy meant confronting a brutal reality: that I needed something more tangible, more human, than prayer.
Admitting I needed help meant admitting that just breathing wasn't living, and I wasn't ready to want more than breath yet.

At nineteen, my beliefs about myself weren't really beliefs; they were carefully constructed survival strategies; I didn't have a self, just a silhouette that shapeshifted to match the threat level, even when the danger was imaginary, or already over.
Danger wasn't always real, but my body never got the memo. I'd spent so many years mastering invisibility, perfecting silence, camouflaging my needs to match whatever the room required.
Romantic love was alien; I'd never even touched it. Restrictions and chaos had robbed me of the quiet spaces where desire might gently grow.
How could I imagine being desirable when simply existing felt too complicated, too dangerous?
I knew what was right in theory, but never what was right for me.
Every instinct screamed "stay safe," but my heart led me repeatedly into situations that shattered that safety. I existed to avoid harm, but somehow, I was harm's favourite Airbnb.

Hope stayed in its cage, pacing. Meanwhile, bills didn't care if I was healing or haemorrhaging.
Yet, managing the everyday felt like assembling furniture without instructions, with no clarity on what went where.
And beneath that chaos whispered the constant, nagging question: Was I healing, or just putting glitter on a

wound and calling it progress?

If my life seems chaotic, and if every chapter reads like one trauma tumbling into another, there's a reason.
Science explains it simply enough: trauma reshapes the brain. It carves pathways primed for survival, not for peace or joy.
Dr. Bessel van der Kolk, a trauma researcher, puts it bluntly: "Trauma victims cannot recover until they become familiar with and befriend the sensations in their bodies."
My chaos wasn't accidental. It was predictable.
Trauma had set my life to a rhythm of crisis, of fight-or-flight, leaving me too exhausted, too wired, too lost to savor anything good.
My decisions: impulsive, reckless, desperate, were less about choice and more about an exhausted swimmer grasping at driftwood, praying the next wave wouldn't drown me.

Maybe you're wondering why I kept turning back to faith after it had wounded me so deeply.
Here's the uncomfortable truth: when chaos is your normal, belief, no matter how flawed, offers something stable, a small island in an endless sea.
Even when religion felt like clutching sharp edges, where bleeding was easier to bear than drifting aimlessly.

To outsiders, it probably looked like a highlight reel of bad decisions.
To me, it was CPR with whatever I had left.

So, the real question was never "Why the chaos?"
It was "How could anything else grow from soil this scorched?"

PART 2

CULTURAL BREAK UP

The word *culture* is defined as the ideas, customs, and social behaviours of a particular people or society. But what happens when two cultures collide within the same child?
My parents were both born and raised in a remote, traditional village in Tunisia, where life moved at the pace of old customs and unchallenged beliefs. When they immigrated to France, they brought their world with them, its values, fears, and inherited expectations. But the world I was growing up in was not the one they had come from.
At home, I was immersed in a culture that felt ancient, tightly wound with rules about honour, obedience, and what a girl must not do. Outside those walls, France offered something very different: freedom, individuality, the right to question, to choose. Balancing those two realities; one at home and one beyond our doorstep, created a fracture in my sense of self, before I knew what "identity" meant.
I didn't know if I was supposed to blend, vanish, or fight. I just knew I didn't fit.

My parents worried constantly about my safety, especially because I was a girl. My brothers came and went freely, without curfews or suspicions, but I had to sneak out just to catch a glimpse of the world. That secrecy became my only taste of independence.

But it came at a cost: I found it hard to make lasting friendships or feel like I belonged. I didn't see anyone around me living in a way I wanted to live.
My mother's friends gathered only to exchange gossip, their conversations circling endlessly around who said or did what and why, and I felt like a ghost in their world.
My father, shaped by an older generation's ideals of masculinity, believed respect came from how others saw you, not from how you treated them. He valued his reputation above all else. He often dismissed women as inferior, incapable, too emotional to be taken seriously. In his eyes, being admired mattered more than being kind. That need for validation consumed him, blinding him to his own vulnerability and leaving no room for change.

Even though my parents came from the same cultural roots, they were separated by nearly a generation in age. That twenty-five-year gap between my parents wasn't just measured in numbers, it was measured in silence, in misunderstandings, in all the things they could never quite say to each other. It showed in the way they argued over little things that meant much more. It showed in the way my father would dismiss her ideas before she even finished her sentence, and in the way my mother learned to retreat into quiet bitterness that would later become a loud and unbearable rage outbreak. They didn't just speak different dialects; they spoke in different emotional currencies. And neither had spare change.
He was a child of the 1940s, shaped by the tail end of colonialism, war, and a patriarchal world where men made the rules and women followed them.
My mother came of age in a slightly newer Tunisia, still confined, but with the first cracks of possibility showing through. Her world had whispered about change. His world had punished it. That gap meant they looked at life from opposite ends of a bridge no one had taught

them how to cross.
And I, born in a different country altogether, stood on a third side, one they couldn't see.
This created a quiet war between them; two people shaped by the same soil but weathered by different storms. They clashed often over how to parent, how to love, how to simply live. And in the middle of it all, I stood, trying to make sense of who I was supposed to be in a house divided not just by age or gender, but by time itself.

At the heart of every conflict, every slammed door, every bitter silence, every raised voice, there pulsed a single, relentless rhythm: money.
When my father first met my mother in a remote Tunisian village, he believed he was rescuing her from poverty, plucking her from hardship and bringing her to a better life in France. It was a narrative of salvation he would cling to for years, one that gave him power and purpose. My father never let my mother forget what he believed he had given her. He reminded her often loudly and cruelly that without him, she would still be in that village, looking desperately after a man to save her. That he was the one who "made her someone," as if her worth were something he had the power to bestow. He used the fact that she had gained the French nationality through their marriage not as a symbol of shared life or love, but as a weapon. It became his favourite currency: the proof of her supposed debt to him. If love was a loan, then I guess we were all just defaulting. But hey, I never signed up for the mortgage.

"You'd be nothing without me," he would say, sometimes muttered with disdain, other times hurled like a stone. And over time, it worked. That sentence seeped into her skin. Into mine.

The spoke of her nationality like it was a gift she didn't deserve. A gift that tied her to him with invisible chains.

He made sure she knew that in his eyes, she hadn't earned her place, that he had handed it to her, and could take it back in a heartbeat, at least emotionally.

It's hard to grow up in a home where love is spoken of like charity. Where dignity is conditional. Where belonging is a bargain. Meanwhile, my mother's family spun their own story; one woven with fantasies of abundance and endless opportunity in the West.
They thought France rained gold. That stepping off the plane meant stepping into a wallet.
These illusions collided violently, not only in my parents' marriage but in the wider circle of my extended family. Money: its promise, its absence, its myths, they ignited wars. There were betrayals that cut deeper than words, acts of sabotage dressed as family duties, theft masked as entitlement, and even physical violence that left more than just bruises.

Sadly, this chaos wasn't a rare occurrence. In the world I knew, the mere mention of money could unravel entire bloodlines. Loyalty and love buckled beneath the weight of unspoken expectations and long-held resentments. And though I know this happens in families everywhere, I've seen how, in some corners of Arabic and African cultures, these fractures take on a particularly sharp edge. Pride and survival are tangled too tightly to easily separate.

From early on, I understood this. I had to.

As the eldest child, I couldn't afford the luxury of childhood. With a father often emotionally and

physically absent, and a mother lost in the haze of untreated mental illness, I stepped in where no one else would. I became the anchor. The protector. The quiet judge who had to decipher right from wrong in real time, without a guidebook. I knew who was lying, who was taking too much, who was twisting love into guilt, like an unpaid therapist with a God complex.
I had to learn fast, because it wasn't just about keeping myself safe, it was about keeping my siblings from slipping into the same darkness I saw growing in the corners of our home.

To this day, I still wrestle with a complex relationship with my culture. I'm not talking about the rich flavours of our food, the warmth of our hospitality, the vibrancy of our community, or the resilience that runs like a thread through our stories, I cherish those.
But culture isn't just couscous and weddings. It's also the wounds you inherit before you learn their names. And for me, that inheritance includes wounds that blur the line between tradition and trauma. It's a constant inner negotiation: which parts of me are shaped by love, and which by survival? Which beliefs are mine, and which were sewn into my skin by generations who never questioned the thread?
I still don't always know where the past ends and I begin. But I do know this, there are patterns I refuse to pass on. Love that isn't wrapped in shame. Protection that doesn't feel like a cage. Pride that doesn't require someone else's humiliation.

–

My mother's relationship with her father was laced with tension, steeped in obligation more than affection. He didn't ask for love, he demanded money. A car, to be precise. Proof that his daughter's life in France meant material success he could claim a piece of. What should have been the quiet, steady presence of a father became a constant, looming expectation.

–

I still remember the first time I tried to reach out to him, a little girl full of hope, ready to offer my heart to someone who could call me his granddaughter. I imagined tenderness, pride, maybe even a smile. But his voice was cold, disinterested.

"I don't know you. I don't have a granddaughter. I don't even have a daughter named [my mother's name]."

I froze, the phone still warm against my ear, my heartbeat suddenly too loud in the silence that followed. I had rehearsed this call in my head so many times, imagined him surprised, maybe even softened by the sound of my voice, reaching across distance and years to finally acknowledge me. Instead, I was met with a door slammed shut in the form of a sentence.
I remember pulling the phone away slowly, staring, realizing I would never have what my friends at school have with their grandparents. I was just a child trying to find family in places where family was supposed to be. But what I found that day was the first sharp taste of rejection that didn't come from strangers, but from blood. From someone who was supposed to claim me and instead erased me.

I hung up feeling like I had reached for something sacred and found only air. I wondered, why don't I get the kind of grandfather other children have? The kind that tells stories, keeps candy in his pockets, or pulls you onto his lap with a laugh.

In time, I would come to understand the deeper currents that shaped our family: how love was often suffocated under the weight of poverty, pride, and manipulation. My grandfather had mastered the tools of emotional control: shame, guilt and blackmail. He wielded them like weapons, and in doing so, he taught us all that love was dangerous. That it could be used against you. That offering it might cost more than withholding it.

My mother was the last of six children, an afterthought in a family already stretched thin. Though she still saw them from time to time, she was raised away from their daily lives. Her mother, tired and drowning, handed her off to *her* mother, like a responsibility she didn't have the energy to love. She grew up in a secluded, rural village, raised by someone two generations removed from her time, her world. The rhythm of her childhood was steeped in silence and outdated ways, with no room for softness or the kind of nurturing every child should know.
From the very beginning, she carried a quiet ache, a longing not just for love, but for *a mother*. A mother who could soothe her fears, stroke her hair, hold her through the storm. That ache never left her. And when I was born, her eldest daughter, she finally found the mother she'd always yearned for.
Somewhere along the way, I became what she had lost. Her child, yes, but also her caretaker, her emotional home. I was never quite sure where the boundaries between us began or ended. All I knew was that I had to be what she needed, because no one had ever been that for her.

–

When I was fourteen, my maternal grandmother fell ill with Alzheimer's, and my mother's determination to see

her one last time transcended the barriers of distance and long-standing conflict. Though my mother had been abandoned and labelled an "excess child" by her own parents, given away to her grandmother because she was, in their words, "lonely in her old age", we still embarked on a journey to Tunisia, driven by my mother's fierce love and unyielding will to say goodbye.
Throughout the long ride, my mother kept murmuring the same thing: "My mom, I will give her some yoghurt... she needs to be strong... I will give her some yoghurt." It was as if that simple, everyday food held the power to heal her mother's fading mind.

We arrived at a house I had only ever known through my mother's anguished outbursts. That house wasn't unfamiliar; it was a living museum of her trauma. I'd heard every exhibit before. The air was thick with tension. As she and my uncle stepped out of the car, their hesitant voices collided with an unspoken storm. My siblings and I sat frozen in the backseat, waiting, sensing something was terribly wrong.
Suddenly, chaos erupted inside — shouts, crashing furniture, the sound of a violent struggle. Though I couldn't see what was happening, I recognized my mother's voice, but this time unlike any before. It was not anger or frustration; it was a desperate cry for help. I knew something terrible had occurred. When my mother and uncle finally emerged from the house, battered and bloodied, my heart sank. Her tear-streaked face bore the scars of a brutal confrontation with her father and sister, who had unleashed their fury because she refused to give them money. In punishment, they denied her the simple human right to see her own mother.

The confusion and fear in that car were unbearable. We sat in stunned silence as my mother muttered to herself,

voice trembling with shock: "She stabbed him! Luna, in the back," she whispered urgently, reliving the horror. "My sister stabbed your uncle and beat me... They won't let me see my own mother. My own mother!"
Tears welled in my eyes as I absorbed her heartbreaking words.
"I only wanted to give her some yoghurt... to see her," she said, voice choked with emotion.

On the way back, when we finally reached Tunis city, my mother wasted no time examining my uncle's wounds. I watched, disbelief freezing my spine, as she carefully inspected the injury. How could she have let him drive in this condition? My uncle stayed silent throughout, his stoic face hiding the pain he must have endured. I shivered, imagining what might have happened to my mother had he not been there to shield her. I couldn't help but wonder: maybe that's why he came in the first place. Maybe he knew it wouldn't go well. Maybe they were waiting to unleash their anger, to punish her for defying them.
The thought chilled me, but it also made the violent scene somehow more understandable and inevitable, like a storm everyone could see coming but no one could stop. I tried to organize chaos like it could be alphabetized. So, I overanalyzed every word, every silence, every glance, desperate to find order in the disorder.

Although my uncle's back wounds were thankfully superficial, the sight of blood soaking his clothes is etched deeply into my memory; a stark reminder of the violence we had just endured and a testament to the unyielding strength of family ties, even when battered by adversity.

I share this story because such harsh realities are, sadly, not uncommon in cultures like mine. The way family conflicts are managed can be deeply ingrained, often erupting with a force disproportionate to the trigger, as if every small dispute awakens some primal survival instinct. In the village where my parents come from, these kinds of scandals are almost a normal part of life. A loud scandal is a dialect and everyone speaks it.
My mother often made such scenes in our home in France as well, which shaped how our French neighbours viewed her; as mentally ill, unstable, someone to be pitied or feared. But back in Tunisia, those outbursts are understood differently.
They are seen as a subtle expression of deep, unbearable pain, almost normalized as part of the way people cope with trauma and hardship. A loud scandal in the streets of the neighborhood in France, is just Tuesday in the village.

In this case, my grandfather and aunt, saw my mother's refusal to provide for them as a profound betrayal; a choice to stand with her own family rather than them. The gulf between his judgment and any sense of parental/family love or protection was staggering, it taught me how warped morals and expectations can fracture even the closest bonds.
There are parts of my culture that I find deeply troubling, yet also elements that are beautiful and unique. I'm learning to strike a balance in how I see it all, seeking healing and growth through understanding and wisdom, rather than letting my own wounds dictate the path I walk. But it's a journey that demands time and patience, as I refuse to let my pain shape how I view life or my culture, just as I wished my mother could have seen beyond her own deep-rooted trauma. Yet, when I linger too long trying to unravel my mother's past and the reasons behind her actions, I feel almost disloyal to

my pain, like by understanding her, I excuse her. And if I do the digging, maybe she never had to. I have become a protector without someone to protect me, loving others without ever feeling truly loved in return. Stuck in survival mode, always on edge, bracing for the next threat. It's a way of existing that keeps me from fully living in the present, forever exhausted by dangers lurking just beyond the horizon.

This hypervigilant half-life, I carry it everywhere. And it's no way to live.
And this is not a state I am willing to settle for.

–

In this memoir, I am reclaiming my voice, and with it, my life. I'm choosing to carve out a new path not only for myself but for my daughter, the way I once longed for my mother to do for us.
Where pain once dictated my steps, I now try to lean into agency. I no longer accept the narrative written for me by trauma, silence, or culture. Instead, I embrace the power of conscious choice; the quiet, radical act of saying: *this ends with me.*
Change begins the moment we stop waiting to be saved and start writing the story ourselves.

For too long, I lived beneath the weight of inherited pain. But now, I stand at a turning point. I understand that true freedom doesn't come from others, it rises from within. It comes from the willingness to face what haunts you, to tend to the wounds, and to rise from them whole.

This is not just a journey of survival. It is a journey of becoming. Of shaping a life defined not by what I endured, but by what I chose to build after.

If my words offer anything, let it be permission to begin again, to feel it all, to want something gentler than what you were given.
We each carry within us the ability to shift the course of our lives. To break inherited cycles. To write new endings. To live truthfully, purposefully, and with love.

We are not the hands that hurt us.
We are the ones we extend in their place, trembling, open and stubbornly kind.
We *are* the quiet, relentless fight to become something more.

PART 3

THE LOCKSMITH

I started experimenting early. My first suicide attempt was at age nine, because apparently, I was precocious even in despair.

At first, it was more ritual than risk; less about dying, more about rehearsing what it might feel like to disappear. But with time, the gestures sharpened.
It wasn't death I longed for. It was the stillness that might follow a body finally unplugged from its siren. My brain didn't yet call it trauma, but my nervous system was fluent in it. The scarf wasn't my last exit strategy, just the first one with a timestamp.
The rest blurred together, with each attempt quieter, less theatrical, more procedural. Like perfecting a scene in a play where the curtain never quite fell.

The longing for the "other side" wasn't about rebellion or melodrama. It was a distress call disguised as silence, because in my world, asking for help got you punished, not protected. And so, it became a quiet wager: I'll shut it all off. My thoughts. My body. The pain. If I can't stop it, I'll stop myself. Survival wasn't some glowing virtue.
It was often accidental, or worse: an inconvenience.

For a long time, it became a daily decision: *I won't do another day of this. I'll shut it all off. My mind, my body. The pain is too much and if I can't stop it, I'll stop myself.*

I see it clearly now: I never wanted death. I wanted the pain to shut the hell up. And that's not just poetic—it's clinical. Research shows most people who attempt suicide aren't seeking death itself. They're seeking relief from something far more relentless: emotional agony with no off-switch. Psychologist Edwin Shneidman, the godfather of suicidology (yes, that's a real field), called it "psych ache", a pain so consuming it convinces the brain there's no other way out but *off*.

Children and adolescents are especially vulnerable. Research in *JAMA Pediatrics* confirms what many of us lived: adverse childhood experiences, like abuse, neglect, growing up in emotional landmines, make you far more likely to try to escape life later. Not out of weakness, but because no one gave your nervous system a break. Or a guidebook.

When trauma goes unrecognized and untreated, the brain adapts to survive rather than thrive—often resulting in dissociation, chronic hypervigilance, and a sense of persistent despair.

And when a child is met not with support but with denial, blame, or gaslighting, the risk deepens.

I'm lucky I never succeeded. But it wasn't just luck. It was also a fight I didn't realize I was in; a quiet battle between surrender and some stubborn and aching parts of me that still believed in mornings.

I remember the moment everything shifted. One minute, I wanted out. The next, I was panicking to stay. Not because I changed my mind, but because my body did. The primitive, terrified animal in me clung to life like it suddenly remembered it had something to live for. It didn't. But instinct doesn't ask questions. It was a terrifying, clarifying moment.

Perhaps it was just instinct, the most primitive part of me reaching for life. That moment may very well have saved me.

While I count myself incredibly fortunate, many others — children and adults — weren't as lucky. Each year, countless lives are lost to suicide, often due to a lack of timely mental health support, fear of being judged or rejected, and perhaps most tragically, the absence of internalized self-worth or love.

Suicidal ideation isn't a rational visitor.

Research shows that when someone is experiencing intense suicidal thoughts, the prefrontal cortex — responsible for decision-making and impulse control — often goes offline. The result is a tunnel vision where the only perceived solution is to escape the pain. There's **no room for reflection** on long-term consequences; survival instinct becomes distorted. As noted in studies from the *American Foundation for Suicide Prevention* and *National Institute of Mental Health*, suicidal crises are often acute and temporary, but tragically fatal when acted upon. That's why the way we talk to someone in crisis is so critical.

Telling a suicidal person to "stay alive for others" may seem well-meaning, but it can unintentionally add additional guilt and pressure. Instead, what research in trauma-informed therapy and suicide prevention recommends is **affirming the person's inherent worth**, reminding them of their light, not their burden.

So, if someone you love is falling through the cracks, don't hand them a guilt-trap disguised as comfort. Instead, say something scandalously radical like: *You matter.* Not because of what you do. Not because of who needs you. But even in your pain, your presence reshapes the room. Your existence is not a burden. It's a goddamn miracle.

These aren't just comforting words.
They can be lifelines.

When someone is drowning in darkness, a glimpse of how deeply they are loved — without condition — can be enough to pull them back toward life. Not because they fear the pain their absence might cause, but because they begin, however faintly, to feel that their *presence* is a source of love and meaning.

Supporting someone in suicidal crisis is emotionally brutal. It's like trying to hold someone up while sinking yourself—but sometimes that hand, even if trembling, is the thing that keeps them from slipping all the way under. And amid that difficulty, one truth stands above all: **hope is essential**.
When someone is drowning in despair, they are not looking for solutions, they are searching for a reason to keep holding on.
Hopelessness can feel like a weight pressing down on every part of their being. The most important thing we can offer is not perfect advice or polished words, but our *presence*. A calm, caring presence can be a lifeline, like a quiet reminder that the world hasn't entirely given up on them.

Often, when trying to help, people reach for well-meaning arguments. They might say things like, "You can't do this to your family," or "Think about all the people who love you." These words often come from a place of deep care, but in a suicidal state, where perception is distorted by pain, such messages can sometimes be received as pressure or guilt.
When everything feels black and white, *some days words matter more than intentions, and on others, intentions matter more than words.* It's hard to predict what will resonate, and that's why listening is so powerful.
What matters most is that we meet the person where they are, not where we wish they were.
Rather than trying to talk them out of their feelings, we

can sit with them in their pain and gently reflect that **there is more beyond this moment**, even if they can't see it yet.

And sometimes, being present also means recognizing our limits. Supporting someone who is suicidal can be emotionally overwhelming. That's not a sign of failure; it's a sign that professional help is needed. Therapists, crisis teams, and suicide prevention hotlines are trained not only to support the person in distress but to support the supporters too.

We're not meant to carry anyone's entire weight, but we can stand beside them until their legs remember how.

Hope isn't loud. It whispers. Sometimes it sounds like your own voice, muttering: *not today, darkness. I've got shit to do.*

From the outside, sure, suicide looks like a puzzle no one wants to solve. But I've lived inside that storm, and I've learned this: Hope is the key. Love is the locksmith. And love doesn't barge in with a sermon; it knocks quietly. Sits down. Says nothing. And stays.

And when love turns the key, the door to despair starts to open.

Through that opening, light begins to enter.

With time, your thoughts become clearer, and your will to live begins to return.

Even in the darkest corridors of despair, I promise, that door *can* open.

And when it does, when even the smallest ray of light breaks through, it's only a matter of time before clarity, reason, and the will to keep going begin to return.

Not in a blaze of glory, but slowly, like dawn through blackout curtains. Even in your darkest hallway, there's a door. And even if you can't open it, sometimes — if you wait just a little longer — someone on the other side will

PART 4

THE TROJAN HORSE

Chapter 1

***(Names are changed to conserve anonymity)**

I spent most of middle and high school floating on the fringe, orbiting social groups I could never quite land in. I didn't date boys. I wasn't allowed to go out at night. House rules read more like solitary confinement than parental guidance. Naturally, that didn't make me the most popular kid to invite to parties — or anywhere, really.

Sanna was one of the few friends I managed to make in middle school, the kind of girl everyone liked without trying. And through her, I met her cousin Nadia, whose life felt like a mirror smashed on the same floor as mine: different pieces, same chaos. There was something about her fragility that pulled me in. A softness sharp enough to hurt if you touched it wrong.

Her vulnerability mirrored mine, like looking into a cracked mirror: familiar but warped at cruel angles.

With Nadia, I felt what I often felt with my mother: the urge to step inside her skin and absorb the pain. Empathy so overgrown it blurred into self-erasure. I looked up to her, tried to support her, even when she

didn't ask. Especially then.
It was as if a silent bond formed between us, anchored by our shared pain. But it was more than empathy; I also admired her resilience. As the older cousin, she carried a wisdom and strength I looked up to, even as I tried to be a source of support for her. Slowly, we began to see each other more and more.

In 2014, when Israel launched an offensive on Gaza, my feed turned into a horror reel, with constant graphic images and grief that sounded too familiar. Add Assad, France, the U.S., Russia, and suddenly everyone had blood on their hands. I watched it all.
I couldn't stop, and bearing witness became my moral currency. As a teenager, witnessing the suffering of innocent children, women, and men unsettled me deeply. I couldn't turn away, I felt an urgent need to bear witness, to not let their pain go unnoticed. After all, this had become my existence, protecting others, witnessing their suffering, offering them unconditional support without asking for anything in return. I was giving what I had never been given.

I remember the dead children most. They became symbols, then obsessions. My own childhood trauma refracted through theirs. I wasn't just heartbroken. I was activated.
Being highly impressionable, I felt a fierce urge to act. Looking back now, I realize my intense determination stemmed from a profound connection to those children caught in war; a reflection of the anguish I experienced at home, *feeling alone and unsupported.*
The injustice they endured struck a deep chord within me, igniting a fierce sense of purpose.
Just as I longed for someone to reach out to me in my darkest moments, I wanted to be that beacon of hope for those who had no one else to turn to.

In their pain, I found my calling, a calling born from the empathy of shared suffering.
At fifteen, I created a Facebook page to vent the chaos I couldn't name. My first video went viral. I had no plan, just a cracked voice and a Wi-Fi connection. It felt like it mattered. But deep down, I knew likes weren't bandages. I needed to *do* something. But what?
Here I was, a French teenager, making videos about something far bigger than herself. I spent most of my time alone in my room, glued to my phone, with few close family bonds and only a handful of real friends.
I could see that what I was doing wasn't really helping the children I saw being murdered on my screen.

I needed to do more. But what?

–

The more I watched, the more I hated. Assad, Israel, the West, injustice itself; it all became one faceless villain. I marinated in outrage, and like any good recipe, it cooked something irreversible. I couldn't look away. But each click was a descent.
As time passed, I noticed Nadia changing, not just in how she dressed, but in how she spoke and carried herself. Sometimes she wore long, dark skirts; other times, she covered her head with a hijab, a new look for her. Then came the niqab, a veil that hid everything but her eyes. But she only wore it occasionally, which made her transformation even more mysterious.
None of these changes seemed to faze Sanna.
One day, the four of us: Sanna, her little sister, Nadia, and I, were hanging out in Sanna's bedroom.

While I plucked Sanna's eyebrows, Nadia suddenly said it was haram, forbidden by the Prophet. I was confused,

because Nadia used to do it too. Then I noticed: her eyebrows were growing out.
Nadia was glued to her phone the whole time, and suddenly a video caught her attention. With a grin, she lifted her phone so eagerly to show us that it unplugged itself from the charger with the enthusiastic movement of her arm and said, "Look, that's the kind of man I want to marry, a real fighter." It was a video of an ISIS fighter holding a severed head high in the air. I don't remember Sanna's reaction, but I remember feeling utterly shocked.
Nadia casually demonstrated how to decapitate a man using just her thumb and a bit of imagination. Nothing screams girlhood quite like a live-action beheading tutorial while someone gets their eyebrows plucked.

That video was from a propaganda piece made by the terrorist group.

Later that day, when I got home, I searched for it, and what I saw challenged everything the media had shown. It depicted a seemingly perfect Muslim society, one ruled by justice and compassion, with men protecting their families. At first, something about that vision resonated deeply within me. But as time passed, I found myself sympathizing with the brutal retaliation they carried out against the regime's army; a harsh, yet, in my eyes then, a justified revenge for the suffering inflicted, especially on the children. Their faces haunted me.

And then Nadia suggested a way we could directly help, the orphans left behind in that so-called perfect Islamic state. Maybe we could be a part of something meaningful, helping those who had lost everything in the war.

Looking back, I realize my attraction and simultaneous fear toward this extremist ideology were rooted in psychological mechanisms well-documented by researchers. According to studies on radicalization, individuals who experience trauma, social isolation, or a profound sense of injustice are more vulnerable to extremist narratives that offer identity, purpose, and belonging (Horgan, 2008; Borum, 2011). These narratives often present a black-and-white worldview, appealing to the emotional need for clarity amid chaos (Doosje et al., 2013).

At the same time, fear and ambivalence arise from the recognition of the violence and moral consequences inherent in such ideologies, activating internal conflict between *attraction to belonging* and *repulsion at brutality* (McCauley & Moskalenko, 2011).

This tug-of-war can create a powerful psychological pull; both compelling and frightening, drawing someone deeper into the worldview even as they remain aware of its dangers.

In my case, witnessing the suffering of innocent children mirrored my own unresolved pain, creating an emotional resonance that made the extremist vision initially appealing. But the harsh reality of their violence and the fear it inspired never fully left me. This tension is common in pathways to radicalization and explains why many youths feel both drawn to and terrified by extremist groups.

I began fantasizing about a new life, not because I believed in violence, but because I was starved for meaning. If I couldn't fix the screaming inside my own house, maybe I could fix the silence outside it. Maybe I could save *someone*. Anyone.

A life surrounded by people who might truly understand me, who shared my deep conviction to help those in need. Above all, I wanted to help the children, no matter how the Islamic State dealt with traitors. I longed to leave everything behind and travel to Syria with Nadia.

–

When Charlie Hebdo happened in 2015, I was too far gone to flinch. Most Muslims around me said the cartoonists got what they deserved. I nodded. I didn't even question it.
One day in high school, during a French class dedicated to practicing debate skills, I expressed these thoughts. The exercise required us to argue against our own beliefs. The Muslims in class argued against portraying the prophet, while others defended it in the name of free speech. No one suspected the depth of my radicalization; outwardly, I showed no signs. I was so deeply entrenched in my convictions that I couldn't even entertain arguing against them.

After the debate, my professor grew concerned and reached out to the school director, who then contacted my parents to share the troubling remarks I had made. When confronted at home, I fiercely denied everything. The school (being a private Catholic institution) handled the situation differently. The director sent me to the pastoral office, where I met with a woman serving as a spiritual guide. Her office was filled with religious icons and Bible verses, and her gentle demeanour struck me as almost disarming. Throughout the meeting, I stayed silent, keeping my thoughts locked away.

In those turbulent times, I felt torn in two; a war raging inside me between opposing souls. One wanted redemption. The other wanted to punch something. Both needed therapies.

Outwardly, I was calm, fearless, sharp-tongued. Inwardly, I was one punch away from collapse.
I wasn't a threat; I was a girl-shaped scream with nowhere to go. It was as if I danced with death without care, already resigned to its embrace long before Nadia entered my life. Yet, beneath that facade lay a hidden truth; a realm of quiet pain where a shattered little girl still lived. In my soul, I wrestled with hopelessness, already convinced that my fate was sealed.
It was a silent war between light and darkness, between the will to survive and the pull of surrender. While the world saw defiance, inside me a much smaller voice cried out, one that had long accepted a destiny shaped by suffering.

A few days later, I returned home from school as usual. Worn down by the endless battles at school, I reached for a book, seeking refuge in the quiet comfort of white pages, craving just a moment of peace. Peace didn't meet me, chaos did. The quiet kind that you learn to fear because it always comes before the scream.
Then came the sound that shattered it: my brother's cry, sharp and anguished. A chill ran down my spine. My feet moved, but everything inside me begged to run the other way.

In the bathroom, I found them: my mother and brother, frozen in a scene of chaos. Her face was twisted in panic, her voice cracking with desperation as she waved a broken wooden broom. A perfect metaphor, really. Worn down, sharp at the edge, and always sweeping chaos.

“I think I broke his ankle!” she sobbed.

Without a word, I turned away and walked to the kitchen, each step heavy with something I couldn’t name. I opened the freezer and scooped out an ice pack, my hands moving automatically. I felt nothing. Just the cold.

“Don’t tell your father,” She begged from behind me. “He’ll kill me!” I didn’t look back. My voice, when it came, was barely a whisper; flat, emotionless, as though it belonged to someone else.

"You shouldn’t have hit him to begin with," I said quietly, my voice flat. I handed the ice pack to my mother and walked away, heading straight to my room. The same heavy feeling returned, like it always did, pressing down on me.

Once I closed the door, I could still hear my mother trying to convince my brother not to show any signs of pain.

In the past, I would’ve stormed out.
Furious.
Yelling: *If you hadn’t hit him, there’d be nothing to hide.*

No bruises to explain.
No limp to deny.

This time, I didn’t storm out. I didn’t even flinch.
I lay there, burnt out like a socket that had sparked too many times. You don’t shout when you’re that tired. You just dissolve. No tears. Just the kind of tired that feels like cement inside your bones. My sadness didn’t explode, it

sank in quietly, like a heavy weight pulling me under. I was so tired. Not just from that day, but from everything. From always feeling like this.

And as I lay there, numbness pressed in from every side. My chest felt empty. My limbs, heavy. My thoughts, distant. My soul, restless.

I couldn't live like this much longer.

"What's the plan? Dow we even have one?" I texted Nadia, the only person I still felt tethered to.

But no answer came.

She stopped coming to school. Vanished. And just like that, I was alone again, adrift in the silence she left behind. Loneliness wrapped itself around me like a second skin. I didn't know who I was without her. Nadia had become my compass in a world without maps, and now I was spinning again.

Just that I was lost. Utterly, painfully **alone.**

Once again.

–

Chapter 2

2016

By 2016, I had over half a million followers. They saw a fearless teen challenging injustice. They didn't see the bruised girl behind the screen, hiding from her mother's screams, preaching hope while choking on it. My content reaches francophone countries around the world, connecting with people of all ages; older viewers surprised by the passion of a young girl speaking about global issues, and younger ones who see in me a role model who looks like them. If only they knew who I really was, how it looked like at home. They had no idea that this teenager trying to defend the oppressed was oppressed herself, inside and out.

One evening, my mother came home from work carrying a box of books that the teachers at the school where she worked in the canteen had given her; books they no longer needed. Inside that box, among other things, I found something unexpected: a Bible. At first, I felt confused and frustrated. Why would she bring that book into our home? It felt foreign and strange to me, like she didn't understand how impure it was.

The Bible sat on my shelf like a dare. I hated it for reasons I couldn't articulate. Which, for a girl who prided herself on overthinking, was suspicious.

I loved books, they were my only real escape, and the fact that I felt afraid or repulsed by one didn't sit right with me. So, I didn't throw it away. I placed the Bible on my shelf, and a quiet curiosity began to grow. Embarrassingly, I realized how little I knew about Christianity. But trapped by the beliefs I'd adopted, I was too afraid to open it, too convinced it was something impure, something unworthy of attention.

Amid my daily routines, the Bible faded from my mind. Spending time with Sanna, lost in video games, gave me a rare moment of calm away from the chaos around us. But beneath it all, thoughts of Nadia stayed with me, a question I couldn't shake: Was she trying to save me... or recruit me?

Then one day, out of nowhere, I found out Nadia had gotten married.
It hit like a punch I didn't see coming. Like her silence had been a warning I ignored.

How? When? Why? Wait... What?
Sanna explained it was a religious ceremony, not a legal marriage recognized by the authorities. Suddenly, everything started to make more sense, explaining Nadia's long absence. I was called to a somewhat secret meeting at Le Suquet, a high point overlooking Cannes. There, I sat beside Nadia and a man whose presence made me uneasy. Nadia spoke passionately about the virtues of a life devoted to Allah and living under Sharia law. I nodded along, but inside, I felt restless and unsure. Underneath her confident words, something felt off. Nadia's sudden change and intense devotion raised alarm bells in my mind.
I wanted to speak up but stayed quiet, much to her frustration. Her husband, quiet and watchful, seemed to agree with her, their words weaving together like two parts of the same plan. But I couldn't shake the feeling that things weren't as they appeared. And despite my growing unease, I was desperate to escape my own life. I ignored the warning signs and threw myself into this unknown path, driven by a reckless hope. Their easy connection, the way they finished each other's sentences, reminded me too much of the recruitment videos ISIS played on repeat. It made me even more suspicious. It became clear that Nadia's marriage wasn't just about love. It was a calculated move: by marrying, she had found a way to enter Syria without needing to wed a stranger there.
Call it Jihadist logistics.

The details of that meeting now blur in my memory, slipping away like sand through my fingers. All that remains is a vague sense of hidden plans and mixed emotions, lost in the noise of everything I was feeling.

–

Despite my deep-seated contempt for the Bible, I couldn't shake the feeling that I had kept it for a reason. As I thought about leaving France with Nadia, trying to ignore my growing suspicions, I realized that no matter where I went, I would still carry this restlessness inside me. And a nagging curiosity lingered at the edges of my mind: why did I hate this book so fiercely? It struck me that I had never even cracked open a Bible before, yet I accumulated such intense hostility toward it. The realization unsettled me; I prided myself on being open-minded and curious, eager to learn and explore new ideas. And here I was, harbouring a blind prejudice against something I knew nothing about.

I mean, books were my oxygen, my lifeboats, my silent witnesses when no one else was watching. But this one — this Bible — felt radioactive; like enemy propaganda wrapped in leather binding. Still, I didn't throw it out. I shelved it. And with that small act, a hairline fracture formed in the fortress I'd built around my beliefs.
The characters in books had always been my only consistent friends — messy, flawed, and blessedly fictional. But the Bible? It wasn't a story; it was a threat. It stood for everything I claimed to hate; hypocrisy, blind faith, colonial arrogance. I despised it so much, I was almost afraid of touching it. Which should've been a clue.

The hypocrisy hit hard. I thought I was open-minded, well, turns out I just liked ideas that didn't scare me.

One night, curiosity shoved fear out of the way.

I picked it up. Heavy. Loaded. Like it knew I wasn't just opening a book, I was opening a door I wouldn't be able to close.

So, with a sense of anxiety, as I opened its pages, I was struck by the realization that there were two distinct testaments: the Old Testament and the New Testament.

I needed guidance on how to approach the Bible.
So, I did what any spiritually conflicted teen would do: I Googled "How to read the Bible".
The search results led me to a chapter called "Matthew."

Intrigued, I began to read.

PART 5

It is well with my soul

Chapter 1

As I opened the Bible, I was greeted by what felt like the world's oldest family reunion; Abraham, Isaac, Jacob... names I'd heard before, but in Arabic: Ibrahim, Ishaq, Yaqub. I hadn't realized these figures lived in both books. Suddenly, the Bible and the Quran were... cousins? It was like realizing your sworn enemy shares your DNA. Unscttling, but fascinating.
I pushed through the genealogy like a determined archaeologist, hoping something less biblical and more relatable was coming.

After making my way through the genealogy, I came across the familiar story of Jesus' birth. Though I had heard it many times before, reading it directly from the Bible gave it a new clarity. The language was simple, the story straightforward, almost like a children's storybook.

I found myself battling with a powerful ambivalence in my feelings. On one hand, I knew I wasn't supposed to like the Bible because it contradicted everything I had been taught. And yet, as I dived deeper into its pages, I couldn't help but feel drawn to it.

Reading the Bible was a forbidden fruit, something I wasn't supposed to do. And there I was, turning its pages and immersing myself in its words. It was a paradox, I shouldn't have liked it, and yet I did. I wasn't supposed to read it, and yet I couldn't resist its allure. There was something about those words; an unspoken magnetism, a quiet power that stirred something inside me I hadn’t fully understood. It was as if the story spoke not just to my mind, but to some hidden part of my soul, calling out to a truth I had long buried, avoided: unconditional love.

With each passing day, I grew more fascinated with the story of Jesus, a figure of unparalleled kindness and love. His words spoke to the deepest corners of my being, offering comfort and peace amid the turmoil. As the screams and fights echoed through the walls of my home, I retreated into the sanctuary of the Bible. It became my refuge, a place where I could escape the harsh realities of my world and immerse myself in a narrative of compassion and unconditional love, concepts I had never heard of or experienced before, concepts I only subconsciously searched for. With each turn of the page, I found myself drawn deeper into the story of Jesus. His gentle demeanour and unwavering love were unlike anything I had ever known. It was a revelation, a glimpse into a world where love knew no bounds, where acceptance was unconditional.

How and why this ancient text had such a hold on me, despite everything, I couldn’t yet explain. But deep down, I sensed it was pulling a thread inside me; slowly, delicately, like unravelling a tightly wound knot I didn’t know I’d been built around. The most disarming part? I didn’t need anyone to decode it for me. No scholar. No imam. No whispering holy interpreter. I could just... read it. And I understood. That alone felt subversive.

Even as the words pulled me in, doubt kept dragging its nails down my back. Voices — internal, inherited — screeched that this was Satan's bait. That I was nibbling at the poisoned hook. That curiosity would kill more than the cat. The fear wasn't logical. It was ancestral.

But beneath the paranoia and suspicion, something else stirred. Something quieter. Something hungrier. The Bible wasn't corrupting me—it was feeding a part of me I'd long starved. A part buried beneath performance, perfectionism, and self-erasure. I didn't have a word for it then, but I do now: love. Not the kind you earn. The kind that exists.

Still, there was shame. Still, fear. Because in the world I came from, this wasn't just curiosity. It was betrayal. It was identity treason. It was *apostasy.*

**Apostasy: an act of refusing to continue to follow, obey, or recognize a religious faith.*

After my encounter with the Bible, something shifted between Nadia and me.
No drama. No final fight. Just... drift. Like two people stepping off the same train at different stops.
That book was quiet, worn and quite possibly possessed; it had cracked something open. It didn't just challenge what I believed. It changed the borders of what I thought was real.

One night, I cracked. Kneeling on my carpet, tears spilling like I'd sprung a leak, I whispered into the void: "Who are you? Allah? Jesus? Nothing? ANYTHING?" The words themselves felt criminal. Like spiritual treason. But under the guilt was something rawer: hunger. Not for answers, but for someone to answer. Who had been listening all this time? And who was whispering back now?

Then came March 9th, 2016. I was just a girl on a bus, zoning out, when suddenly... it landed.
A quiet, immovable truth:
I believed. Jesus was the Son of God.
No dramatic conversion montage. No choir of angels. Just a quiet click inside me, like something had fallen into place behind my ribs.
And then panic.
Wait... me? A Christian?
A girl who once felt rage just looking at a Bible?
I felt exposed and terrified. But beneath it all —beneath the fear of what this meant for my body, my home, my future — was something gentler. Peace that holds your hand in a storm and doesn't let go. The kind that whispers, *this is yours now.*

In my search for truth, or maybe just some kind of divine clarification, I wandered into a Catholic church.

Okay... "Wandered" is generous. I *snuck* in. It felt like theological trespassing. Like God might peer down from heaven, spot me kneeling under a crucifix, and yell, *wrong house, kid.*
But I went anyway. Because something inside me needed answers. Or maybe just a space where no one would scream at me for asking questions. But curiosity pushed me forward.
Inside, it smelled like melted wax and centuries of whispered guilt. I watched as a group of sweet old ladies clutched what looked like pearl necklaces and prayed to the Virgin Mary like she had office hours.
I liked them. But also, my theology alarms were ringing.
"Isn't there a verse... 1 Timothy something... about there being only one mediator between God and humans — and it's not Mary?" I asked the priest, trying not to sound smug.
He smiled politely. I left confused, but with better posture.

"Wait... isn't there a verse somewhere... yeah, 1 Timothy 2:5, about there being only one mediator between God and humans, and that being Jesus?" I asked the priest, present with the ladies. I left with more questions than answers. I had this fantasy of stumbling into a Book of Acts kind of church; tight-knit, on fire, breaking bread, casting out demons over dinner. What I found felt more like a historical reenactment. I was the awkward visitor trying to decode a 1,700-year-old secret handshake.
So, I kept searching.

Next stop on my spiritual tour: a Protestant pastor. Our talks were rich, kind, full of wisdom. I was a sponge with abandonment issues, soaking it all in.

But something felt off. Their faith was... polite. Trimmed. Pressed. Mine was feral. On fire.

I didn't want quiet assurance; I wanted people who worshipped like their hearts were breaking open and stitched back together in the same breath.
Then came the non-denominational church. Or maybe it came for me. It was vibrant, loud, gloriously unfiltered. Evangelical, technically — but I didn't care about labels. The worship was messy and alive. People prayed like they meant it and confessed like they knew grace. Loved like it wasn't embarrassing.

I found my people.

I made real friends. The kind who didn't recoil when I told them my mess. The kind who prayed like it mattered, who texted me Bible verses like little guided missiles of encouragement. I laughed. I cried. I sang terribly. And no one cared. I didn't have to guard every inch of myself. I was part of something, something real.

Of course, being a Christian in secret started feeling like a spiritual double life. I was basically undercover, but Jesus edition. No gadgets. Just guilt. I hid my Bible like it was contraband. I tiptoed out the door like I was going to a rave instead of a worship night. And eventually, I knew it had to stop. If faith was real, it had to be seen.

So, I did the unthinkable: I decided to tell my family.

Naively, I believed they might understand. Maybe they'd even be curious. Maybe we'd read the Bible together, cry, and start a little house church!

Yeah, I was dreaming big.

I started with my dad. I figured he'd be the most open-minded of the bunch, especially when it came to religion. But, well... let's just say that assumption aged like a banana in the sun.

I came home from church with a knot in my stomach and a plan that felt like walking into traffic. I called my father into my room.

"Can you close the door?" I asked. He looked confused but obeyed, sealing us both into a space now charged with spiritual explosives.

"I need to tell you something," I said, my voice a thin thread. "Please don't be angry. I'm happy."

Deep breath.

"I've decided I'm no longer Muslim. I'm a Christian now."

The air thickened like soup. And just like that, I detonated the room.

He stared.

No words.

No explosion.

Just... silence.

Then he turned around, walked out, and closed the door behind him like I was a bad thought he didn't want to finish. I sat there frozen. Maybe he needed time. Or maybe, I had just become a ghost.

I picked up my Bible like it was a flotation device. I flipped to the parts I remembered; the ones about rejection, betrayal, family turning on you. Jesus had warned me. He didn't sugarcoat it.

He never said it would be easy. But he also never said I'd have to do it alone. And that helped. A little.

The afternoon dragged in a silence so dense it felt like

the house itself had slipped into mourning. My father said nothing. Not a "hmm," not a grunt. Honestly, I'd have preferred a rage monologue, a door slam, a dramatic "you've disgraced us all!" moment. Instead? Just the clink of cutlery during dinner like we weren't living in a slow-motion spiritual crisis.

By dinner, the atmosphere had gone from tense to apocalyptic. It wasn't an elephant in the room, it was the whole zoo, and everyone pretended not to notice while politely chewing their food like we weren't mid–spiritual crisis. No one spoke. Everyone chewed like it was a tactical operation. I gave up, retreated to my room, and tried to make peace with hunger.

Eventually, my stomach staged a protest, and I crept out to the kitchen like a ghost on a snack mission.

And that's when they jumped me.

My youngest brother grabbed my arms like we were filming a budget fight scene for a movie no one would watch. My other brother decided this was his audition for the role of "angry fists." No warning. No words. Just impact.

I didn't even get a chance to scream, because what I saw next numbed me more than the blows.

My parents were still on the couch, watching TV.

Not in horror. Not in confusion.

Just... watching.

Like they were trying to decide if what was happening was part of the show or just a commercial break.

Apparently, the sight of two of their sons pummelling their daughter in the living room didn't warrant a channel change. That's when it hit me: I'd officially crossed the line from *family member* to *background character.* Maybe even a guest star on their evening drama, except I hadn't been told my scene involved stunts.

That night, I didn't eat. Not because someone told me not to, but because they didn't have to. The kitchen felt radioactive. The living room might as well have had lasers. At that point, I was just heresy in human form. Just existing in shared air felt like an act of defiance.
So, I stayed in my room, *hungry but safer*, and tried to act like skipping dinner was a choice. My mother did call me to eat sometimes. She didn't want me to go hungry, at least not completely. But whenever I did sit down, it was like walking into a courtroom where the verdict had already been decided. The food might have been warm, but the air was freezing. I couldn't take a bite without being met with sharp insults, long silent stares of contempt, or the unmistakable art of side-eyeing, a family specialty, apparently. It wasn't a meal. It was a performance in humiliation. So, I stopped showing up. Hunger was easier to stomach than humiliation.

Hiding my Bible became a full-time job. Spy-level stuff. I wasn't only reading scripture; I was smuggling it. Under my bed, I carved out what can only be described as a miniature tomb for Jesus. A sacred little bunker, buried beneath laundry and old notebooks, where my Bible could rest in peace... or at least until the next surprise room inspection. But under-bed storage wasn't enough for a spiritual contraband item. I needed backups. Contingencies. So, I diversified. My teddy bear: innocent, fluffy, and dead-eyed, became an unwitting smuggler of the gospel. I sliced open its back, tucked the Bible inside, and sewed it up like some kind of cartel mule. No one ever suspected the bear. He looked soft.

Loyal. Christian, maybe. I also hid it in my clothes cupboard, wedging it between oversized sweaters and the stuff I pretended to wear in public.
At this point, I probably had more hiding places than the average war criminal. But it wasn't paranoia, it was survival. If found, that Bible would've been treated like a weapon of mass destruction. And we know what we do to those suspected of having them.
So, I prayed in whispers. In shadows. Tucked in corners like some underground resistance agent. And weirdly, it gave me strength.

I didn't know what was going to happen next, but I knew one thing for sure: if faith was a crime in that house, I was guilty; and I planned to reoffend.

Chapter 2

From my earliest memories, our family had a tradition: every year, we would embark on a month-long journey to Tunisia, our ancestral homeland. My mother would grind spices; make couscous and other types of Arabic foods she could only get there. These vacations weren't just trips; they were a lifeline to our roots, a chance to reconnect with extended family and soak up the vibrant culture that shaped us. The laughter, the smells, the sounds of Tunisia became woven into the fabric of my childhood. But as the years went by, money grew tight. The trips became fewer and farther between, and the tradition felt like it was slipping away leaving me adrift in a sea of longing and nostalgia.

Then came 2017. Against all odds, my father declared we were going back. The old tradition was alive again, and hope sparked inside me. I was filled with a mix of happiness and anticipation, imagining the familiar sights and sounds that awaited us. As the departure day drew closer, my excitement swelled. I dreamed of reuniting with childhood friends, wandering through streets lined with shops bursting with colours and treasures, everything under the sun, it seemed. I could almost taste the salty sea breeze, feel it tugging at my hair, and smell the rich, earthy spices drifting from market stalls. But more than anything, it was the language that called to me, the lyrical rhythm of Tunisian Arabic, a melody that stirred something deep inside my soul. And as we set off on that journey, I knew that no matter where life might take me, the memories of Tunisia; its people, its places, its language, would always hold a special place in my heart.

Tunisia started out like a dream. Sand, sea, spices—the usual nostalgia hit. But just as I began to exhale into the familiar rhythms of our house in Tunis, my mother dropped her signature brand of chaos:
"You're going to see a healer."
A *witch*, to be precise. Great, now, a spiritual detox.

Her words hit like a thunderclap, shattering the fragile joy I'd clung to since our arrival. There was a mixture of hope and desperation in her voice, and her eyes betrayed the deep worry she tried to hide.

Our relationship had long been strained; full of clashes, aggressive tensions, and unspoken hurts. Every conversation felt like walking on thin ice, where one wrong step sparked another argument. To my mother, my new faith was more than just a difference in belief; it was the last straw, proof that our problems were bigger

than either of us wanted to admit. That trip wasn't a vacation; it was a setup. A showdown between our ghosts. Hers were loud, mine were quieter, but both had packed a suitcase.
And now, my mother was sending me on a pilgrimage to a healer, hoping she could untangle whatever darkness had taken hold of our family.

"A demon?" I wondered, half-joking, half-dreading the answer. "Mom, I'm not sick," I said, my voice sceptical but steady.

"It's not about being sick," she replied. "This woman is good. She'll understand why we can't stand each other and give us a remedy."

I refused categorically, but it wasn't up to me.

We drove to the healer's house — a villa too fancy for the crumbling neighborhood it squatted in.
Inside, the waiting room looked like a casting call for a horror movie that meets psychiatric ward. People rocking, whispering, zoning out. My heart didn't sink; it rolled its eyes. My father whispered tales about her powers, claiming even government officials supposedly trembled at her name. Yeah, sure, sounds legit.

One of the healer's assistants walked up to me with three strings — each knotted with raisins — like she was about to perform some kind of dark culinary magic.
"Swallow these," she said.
I obeyed, naturally, because who doesn't love choking down raisins tied to twine in front of strangers?

The raisins went down. The strings stayed dangling from my lips. As I waited my turn for a face to face with the witch, a cocktail of discomfort and morbid curiosity bubbled inside me. I wasn't scared. If anything, I was determined to see how far this charade would go.

Finally, it was my turn. The room was like a bizarre alchemist's lair, small pots filled with powders, liquids, and mysterious substances in every colour of the rainbow. The smell was oddly pleasant, like walking down the perfume isle in a shop and a science lab gone wrong. I sat down on the elevated chair, facing the healer's imposing throne. My eyes landed on the trash can nearby. What I saw made my skin crawl: animal eyes, tufts of fur, mouse fur, maybe? I wondered if it was part of some ritual or just a gross day at the office. Then, with lightning speed, the healer grabbed the strings from my mouth and yanked them upwards. Instead of the raisins I'd swallowed, a bubble of fur popped out. Fur. Inside me. I blinked. Seriously? What was I? Some walking petri dish? It was absurd, almost comical if it hadn't been so creepy. The whole thing felt like a bad horror movie, except the monsters were raisins disguised as a demon. With an aggressive flick, she tossed the strings into the trash can, the same revolting bin already overflowing with a buffet of bodily rejects: fur tufts, cloudy jars, and unidentifiable organic clumps. That's when it hit me: this trash bin was a communal stomach graveyard. Everyone's spiritual leftovers, dumped into one place like some cursed potluck. I nearly gagged. I wasn't sure if I needed therapy, antibiotics, or both. What was the point of all this? Some grotesque performance art? A magic trick dressed up as a spiritual intervention. Or maybe just a bold business model: extract something disgusting, call it a curse, and charge extra for the trauma.

Then she dropped the line.

"Your parents think you have a Christian demon inside you," she said, deadpan.
I blinked. *A Christian demon.*
That's not a diagnosis; that's a genre twist. I nearly laughed.
"Seriously? Is that what this is about?"

"I am not possessed by no demon. Is that seriously why I'm here?" My voice was dry, partly from disbelief, partly from the scratchy grape-string assault on my throat. It finally sank in: they hadn't given my mother the sacred raisin necklace. This was a one-way exorcism. All of this, every string and chant and potion, was aimed at me. Apparently, I was the plague. The shame. The haunted child needing spiritual pest control. I reached for water, but the healer handed a bottle to my mother instead, some murky liquid with floating herbs, possibly hair, possibly seaweed, who knows. I overheard her whispering instructions: how and when to rub it on me. I was now a cursed roast chicken in need of spiritual marinade.

On our way out, we passed through the waiting room again; and suddenly, the absurdity stopped being funny. It cracked open, and underneath was just... pain. These weren't just superstitious people or spiritual hobbyists. These were people in crisis. People hurting. People desperate enough to swallow raisins on a string because they didn't know what else to do. These weren't just confused people or gullible believers; they were people in pain.
Many were clearly dealing with serious mental health conditions. One little boy sat in the corner, rocking, eyes vacant, hands flapping like butterfly wings in distress. I didn't know what it was then. Now I'm sure—he was autistic. And instead of help, they brought him here. To be healed. Or exorcised. And that's when the anger hit.

Has it ever occurred to this society that mental health disorders are real? Treatable? Manageable? Apparently not. We keep circling back to this toxic belief that mental illness = crazy = cursed. And that belief doesn't just destroy the person who's suffering; it drags down everyone around them. Families fracture. Guilt multiplies. Shame blooms in silence. And in all that desperation and fear, someone saw a business opportunity. There was demand, so someone supplied. Not with help, but with hexes. Not medicine, but mystery. Not compassion, but capitalist sorcery, delivered in the form of raisin ropes and fur bubbles. It was more than heartbreaking. It was infuriating. And no one seemed to question it, because it was easier to believe in demons than to face the terrifying idea that someone you love might just need real help.

In Tunisia, mental illness isn't called by its name. It's whispered about in alleyways, hidden behind curtains, or, in my case, hauled off to a healer who "pulls out" invisible demons with produce and twine. Mental health struggles aren't treated; they're exorcised. Not through therapy or medication, but again, through rituals, charms, potions, and fear. And it's not just fringe belief. Studies show most people there still see mental illness as the result of spiritual punishment or possession.

Psychosis? That's not schizophrenia—it's a jinn. Depression? Maybe you've angered God. Autism? Just bad parenting or a curse.

It's terrifying, not just because it's false, but because it delays treatment. On average, people wait more than a year after symptoms start before seeing a psychiatrist, if they ever do.

Healers thrive in this climate. They feed off desperation and stigma, offering snake oil remedies with spiritual flair. It's not healing. It's theatre. And it works because people are too ashamed to admit their child is sick, too scared of the shame mental illness brings to the family name. So, they turn to someone who offers certainty. A clear villain. A demon. A cure. But mental illness isn't demonic. It's human. It's treatable. It's survivable. And yet here, belief still dictates that being sick means being cursed. That belief doesn't just harm the person who's unwell, it fractures families, ruins lives, and turns genuine suffering into a spectacle.

"Mom, if you bring that potion anywhere near me, I swear I will run to the airport barefoot."
I wasn't kidding. I didn't want it on my skin, my clothes, or within a three-meter radius of my aura.
She looked at me with that unsettling mix of patronizing concern and spiritual warfare readiness.

"We'll see about that," she replied.
"She's an experienced woman," she continued, as if that justified the raisins and fur.
"She told me our relationship is strained because a demon is trying to take you away from me, from us. So run as far as to the moon, and I'll be there waiting for you, because I love you."

That wasn't comforting. That was a threat.
A lunar-level threat.

When we arrived home, my pulse spiked. I opened the door to a scene that looked like a cross between a religious intervention and a low-budget horror film: my dad, my siblings, a few neighbors and two strangers, perched on the couch like they were about to rate the

exorcism on TripAdvisor.
And then... the sheep. Oh... the sheep.
Tied to the terrace. Calm. Innocent. Definitely not in on the plan.
I blinked. *Was this for me? Was I about to be sheep-adjacent to a religious cleansing?*

"Baba... what the hell is this?" I asked, blinking like I'd wandered into the wrong universe.

"This is the imam who will help you," he said, gesturing solemnly. "And this is the healer who will assist him."

Oh, a tag team. How comforting.

I stood there, internally debating whether to scream, cry, or laugh maniacally. I felt like I was being prepped for an exorcism-themed reality show: *Keeping Up with the Confused Apostate*. The imam looked at me with all the warmth of a tax audit, puffed up with pride like he'd just been called to personally save the soul of Satan's favourite. And the neighbours? Smiling. Sipping tea. Watching. Because apparently spiritual coercion is best enjoyed with refreshments.

Why was I a threat? Simply because I had changed. Because I now believed something different? So much for "there's no compulsion in religion." Individuality was clearly dead. I was on trial for thinking independently, and the jury was comprised of extended family, livestock, and unsolicited spiritual consultants.

With my pocket Bible in hand like a tiny sword in a world of pitchforks, I took a seat opposite of the imam and decided to speak.

"My faith won't change. God, if anything, it's stronger now," I said, voice steady. "All of this is unnecessary, you're wasting your time. And more importantly, you're sabotaging my family as if our self-sabotaging wasn't already a full-time job. Trying to exercise authority that, frankly, I don't believe you have.

"So, respectfully," I said, holding my tiny Bible like a mic drop, "why don't you all go home and leave me and my 'demon' alone?" The imam squinted at me like I'd just insulted his beard oil.

"You know, Jesus is also present in Islam..." he began.

"I know," I cut him off. "Yeah. I know. But I'm not here to debate. I'm here to say no. Don't waste your time trying." And try he did. For what felt like hours. He quoted, lectured, guilt-tripped, emotionally blackmailed, all the hits. And everyone else stayed silent, like they were watching a movie with subtitles they didn't understand but didn't dare interrupt.

Eventually, I stopped talking. Not because I lost the argument—because I lost the will to participate.
My brain hit airplane mode. I was there, but I wasn't. Floating above the room, watching my body stay polite while my soul packed its bags.
Finally, the imam turned to my father with a solemn shake of the head.

"Your daughter is gone, and never coming back," he said. "Satan has gotten to her. I'm sorry."

And my father cried.
Not when I was beaten. Not when I begged.
But now.

Because apparently, faith was the true tragedy.
And I sat there dry-eyed, watching the scene unravel.
I didn't feel gone.
I felt suspended.
Half-floating, half-rooted — somewhere between dissociation and defiance.
More aware than ever, and somehow less real at the same time.

But in their eyes, I had already crossed over to the other side, armed with nothing but faith, a paperback Bible, and the refusal to be unmade.

Standing in the middle of it all, I felt... nothing. Or maybe too much. Who knows. My nervous system had checked out like a hotel guest who saw something sketchy on the security camera feed. I was just there, breathing on autopilot, wondering how *being loved differently* had escalated into *spiritual crime scene cleanup featuring live sheep sacrifice.* I wasn't hurting anyone. Was I? In fact, at that point, my faith was probably the best thing that had ever happened to me. I had finally felt unconditional love. The kind that didn't dangle approval like a carrot on a string. And somehow, that made me dangerous?

I was angry. Deeply, blisteringly angry. But under that lava was something sadder: I understood them. Not their choices (those were absolutely unhinged), but the fear behind them. I gave them grace, even when all they gave me was a sheep on death row and a room full of people staging a spiritual intervention like they were on some cursed episode of *Tunisian Ghostbusters*.

Then came the finale.
The sheep was slaughtered. Not for Eid, not for hospitality. For me. To purify the house from my existence, like I was some kind of spiritual mildew.
The blood was meant to wash the walls clean of me.
And the meat? Turned into couscous, my favorite dish; like a peace offering soaked in denial.
A "we love you, but only after we've gutted something" sort of gesture.
Bon appétit.

But I wasn't even allowed inside to smell it. I was the contamination.

I stood outside, barefoot on ceramic tiles, like some biblical leper exiled from the meal that used to mean family.
Inside, they stirred the pot with generational trauma and a bit too much cumin.
I could hear them laughing. Not in cruelty.
Just in... normalcy.
As if nothing had just happened.

I wish I could say I cried. Or screamed. Or flipped the table like a dramatic exit.
But I didn't.
I froze.
My brain turned the lights off. Shut the blinds. Went on lockdown.
That's what trauma does, it doesn't always shout. Sometimes it just disconnects the power and pretends no one lives there anymore. That's the thing about trauma. People think it's dramatic, big, loud, visible. But for me,

it's quiet. It numbs. Meanwhile, my body whispers reminders; stomach cramps, sudden fatigue, random aches, just in case I forget that it *did* happen. And it *did* hurt.

I'm telling this story with humour not because it was funny, but because it's the only way I can write it without breaking into pieces.

Humour is my emotional duct tape. And right now, I'm holding myself together with it.

Because if I ever take the tape off,
I'll have to look at the bruises —or worse, remember how quietly they formed.
After all, laughter is cheaper than therapy, and sometimes, it's the only sound that proves I made it out alive.

–

In the days that followed, my mother chased me around with the witch's mysterious "remedy", a murky bottle that looked like fabric softener and smelled like divine Febreze.
Apparently, spiritual cleansing now came in citrus scent.
Because nothing says holy war like trying to rub detergent on your apostate daughter, huh?
Looking back, the whole scene almost feels like a sketch from a doomed sitcom: my mom chasing me around the house, potion bottle in hand, while I ran for my life like the house was haunted and I was the only one who knew it.

At the time, it wasn't comedy—it was collapse.
Humiliating. Depleting.
A psychological mugging dressed up as maternal concern.
And all I could do was keep running, keep hiding, keep pretending this was survivable.

By then, I didn't care anymore where these beliefs came from; religion, culture, superstition, fear, or some volatile cocktail of all of them. What mattered was that my dignity, my thoughts, my choices — *myself*, were rejected wholesale.

Not because I'd hurt anyone. Not because I'd committed some crime. But because my beliefs didn't fit the script, and the fear of bringing "shame" to the family outweighed love.

The sacred commandments of reputation whispered through every wall:
What will they say? What will the neighbors think?
These weren't just questions. They were laws.
Louder than love. Louder than logic. Louder than the sound of me disappearing. They dictated every move we made. Everything was about controlling the exterior: perform the part, polish the story, keep the mask on. Behind closed doors? Well, that was where the real horror lived.

So, when we flew back home to Cannes, I wasn't exorcised, converted, or spiritually scrubbed clean.

I was still a Christian.

And maybe, more than ever, I knew why.

But something else changed, too. I had seen what happens when faith is hijacked by fear, when love is used like a leash, and God becomes a weapon dressed in concern.
And I knew I'd never follow that version again.
Not even if they bled a hundred sheep for it.

Chapter 3

Looking back, my inner chaos and dramatic pivots weren't that rare. Psychologists even have a name for this kind of existential slingshot: ideological whiplash.

Turns out, when you've clung to one extreme belief system like a life raft in a storm, and that raft starts leaking, the brain doesn't calmly search for a stable canoe.
No.
It cannonballs into the next available vessel, even if it's patched together with emotional duct tape and existential glitter. If it floats, it qualifies.

Psychologists call it "cognitive closure", our brain's refusal to leave questions unanswered. It craves resolution, even if that "resolution" is just a rigid worldview glued together with anxiety and cultural guilt. If the first belief system doesn't meet your inner cravings for meaning or belonging, the brain just scrolls to the next thing on the spiritual buffet. It wants intensity. Simplicity. A strong flavor and a set menu. No ambiguity allowed.
And then there's trauma; the interior decorator of the nervous system. Leave it in fear, chaos, and rejection long enough, especially in childhood, and the brain

starts rewiring itself like a drunk electrician with no permit.

The thinking parts of your brain start outsourcing into the survival parts — the ones that don't care what's true, just what hurts less.
So you don't find safety.
You just find a fire that feels familiar.
Swapping extremes isn't a glitch. It's a coping strategy. One burning building for another, because at least this one says the pain has a purpose.

One illusion traded for another, dressed up in meaning and mercy. I didn't find a lifeboat. I found another wreck, just one that smiled while it sank and told me the water was holy.

PART 6

THE NOT-SO-LAST REFORMATION

Chapter 1

It was becoming painfully clear to my father that my new faith wasn't just a teenage phase, like dying your hair blue or insisting avocado toast is a personality trait. No, this was sticking. And he was losing patience.

September 2017.
I had just returned from a trip to Paris with friends from church. We'd spent the week sharing the Gospel, talking to strangers on trains, praying with people on sidewalks, and occasionally getting politely ignored, which is its own spiritual discipline in France. On the way back, we had a layover in Lyon.

As I reached for my suitcase, my phone rang.

It was my father.

"Where are you? What are these videos your brother showed me on the internet? Are you crazy?!"

His voice came through like a slap. No greeting. No space to breathe. I knew exactly what videos he meant, someone had uploaded clips of our street preaching. I imagined him watching me smiling, testifying about Jesus on some boulevard in Paris, his blood pressure rising with every syllable.

"I'm sorry it made you sad, Baba," I said gently, already sensing where this was going.
"I'm sorry, Baba," I repeated softly, but he cut in before I could say more.
"You either stay Muslim, stick to your roots... or you never come back."
Then the line went dead.
I don't know what I felt. Probably a cocktail of confusion, shock, denial, and numbness... shaken, not stirred. But underneath it all, one thing was clear: I was lost.

Utterly, painfully alone.

Once again.

I stood there, staring at nothing, in an airport that now felt cold in more ways than one. It took me a few minutes to process what had just happened. The gravity of it hit slowly: I was homeless. My home had just been revoked over a phone call. All I had was a half-charged phone, a few euros, and a suitcase full of clothes that suddenly felt way too heavy. No drama. No bags being thrown out onto the street. Just a click, and that was it. A door slammed without ever being touched.

I never had a close relationship with my father. Our conversations were never warm or easy, more like check-ins than heart-to-hearts. He didn't show affection, not the verbal kind, not the physical kind, not any kind, really. He kept his past sealed tight, like a box he'd

thrown into the ocean.
Growing up, I often wondered if he even *had* emotions, or if he'd just decided a long time ago that feeling things was too dangerous. He was my dad, but I didn't really know who he was; not as a man, not as a person.
And yet, his rejection still hit me like a truck.
Because even when you don't feel close to someone, you still quietly hope they'll surprise you with love when it counts. You hope they'll come through.
But he didn't.

One of the friends with me at the airport spotted my "The Scream" painting face, you know that perfect mix of shock, horror, and "What the heck just happened?" After I spilled the story, they could clearly see I was in full-on distress. Without missing a beat, they started scrolling through their phone contacts. Meanwhile, I was desperately trying to find somewhere, anywhere to crash for the night while I scrambled to figure out my next move. Honestly, I don't even remember where I slept that first night. Most memories from that time come back as emotional aftershocks, not images. Blurry outlines wrapped in razor-edged feeling.
What I remember most is the choking sense of rejection, and the way I would start to hyperventilate when I thought about the possibility that I might never see my little sister again. She's nine years younger than me. And what I did to her — leaving without warning — is a wound I still can't touch without flinching. That day at the airport, I left her behind. For my freedom. To survive. I didn't say goodbye. I didn't explain. I just disappeared, and in doing so, I abandoned the one person who looked up to me more than anyone else.

To her, I wasn't just a sister. I was her emotional anchor, her stand-in mom, her safe place. And I left.
I told myself I didn't leave her, I left them. But that line

was imaginary. And children can't read subtext. Only silence.
But the truth is, it didn't matter how I justified it, she lost me too.

And she didn't get a choice.

I still see her brushing her teeth next to me at night, asking me if I thought our mother would be scary tonight. I told her no, probably not. I lied. Now I can't help but wonder: Who will hold her when our father gets physical with our mother? Who will she turn to and whisper, "Is Mommy going to be scary tonight?" Who will play cards with her when she can't sleep? Will she sneak into my room and make it her own? I hope she does. It's the only space in that apartment that isn't hoarded, the only place that ever felt like it could breathe. Who will tell her, "I love you, I see you, I'm here for you" and mean it, and stay? What will she think when she realizes I left, just like that, from one day to the next? And how will she handle it when our parents twist the story, when they tell her I abandoned them all? Because I know how they work. I know their need to rewrite pain into blame.

I need my sister to be okay without me. But I don't know if that's even fair to ask.

–

After that phone call at the airport, I was a mess. Still burning with passion for God, but my mental health was hanging by a thread. The feeling of being utterly abandoned clung to me. After the phone call at the airport, it was a blur of hopping from one stranger's home to another: Christians, thankfully, but still strangers all the same. Basically, I became a professional guest in a very awkward Airbnb circuit I never signed up for but nevertheless, that I was grateful for.

Nightmares haunted my sleep almost every night, like my brain was going through withdrawal from the constant, high-dose chaos of home. Trauma had been my baseline for so long, my nervous system treated peace like a threat and stillness like a trap, but I wasn't really sleeping, more like trapped in a restless limbo, adrenaline coursing through my veins while my body ached for no clear reason.
I wish I could say the pain ended when I left. That once I escaped the walls of that house, that life, that silence, I instantly became whole. That I walked into freedom and never looked back. But healing doesn't work like that. It isn't a doorway. It's a desert. Some days, it felt like all I had done was trade one kind of loneliness for another. I was no longer being screamed at or spiritually ambushed, but I was also not being held. Not by my parents. Not by certainty. Not by anyone who truly knew me. The Christians who once welcomed me with open arms sometimes felt more curious than compassionate. My story was interesting, even inspiring. But I was more than a testimony. I was a person, and that part was harder for people to handle. I didn't just need food and hugs. I needed safety. I needed space to *not* be okay. And yet, there were moments. Tiny ones. A warm plate set in front of me. Someone who let me stay without asking for my story. A quiet walk in the cold, where no one talked, and no one needed to. A room with a door I could lock. These weren't miracles in the biblical sense. But to me, they were everything.

The weight of depression pressed down on me like a prisoner's stone, dragging me into a darkness that swallowed even the outlines of who I was. And still, strangely, there was relief. A soft, forbidden kind of freedom in knowing I might never have to see my family again. No more screaming. No more surprise beating. No more spiritual exorcisms. No more walking on eggshells through the ruins of a house pretending to be a home. But even that came with guilt.

I missed them.
I hated them.
I longed for them.
I feared them.
It was a messy, tangled ache.
I was grieving the loss of something I had never truly had.

And yet, again, I held on.
So, I kept going.
Not with big plans or certainty, but blindly.
Day to day.
Hour by hour.
Minute by minute.

That was enough.
That had to be enough.

I began to realize that healing wasn't about finally feeling good.
It was about feeling *real.*
Feeling everything.
Anger.
Numbness.
Shame.
Hope.

And not abandoning myself in any of it.

Yes, they made me choose between obedience and survival. And I chose survival. But now I'm building a life loud enough for my little sister to find me.

Chapter 2

One day, while staying at yet another stranger's home, my host invited me to join a Christian seminar, in Montpellier. It was run by a group of Danish people who proudly claimed to live exactly like the early Christians in the Book of Acts did. That was almost their slogan: "Faithful to the Book of Acts." It sounded promising, like something real and raw. After all, this is what I've been searching for since I read the New Testament.

When we arrived at the location, I was surprised by how beautiful the house was; spacious, clean, and oddly cozy, like a giant Swiss cottage plucked out of a snow globe and dropped into real life. It had that "Pinterest Christian retreat" vibe: brown stone floors, natural light, and absolutely zero hoarding in sight. My nervous system was both impressed and suspicious.

Inside, the place was buzzing. There were a lot of people. Some were Christians, some weren't, but most had that hopeful, slightly nervous look on their faces, like they were at a spiritual version of a talent show, waiting to see if a miracle would appear. I came to understand that this group had developed a bit of a reputation. Miracles were their thing. They didn't just talk about Jesus, they went full Book of Acts: healing, casting out demons, street baptisms, you name it. I had never seen anything like it. Up until that point, my Christian experience was mostly emotional worship, passionate preaching, and the occasional potluck. But this? This was action. And I was intrigued. Curious. Maybe even a little too eager. After all, their name: *The Last Reformation*, was an action name. It sounded less like a church and more like a sequel no one asked for.

We took our seats, lined up in tidy rows, and the seminar began. There was a whiteboard up front, and a young man named John stepped forward to speak. He had the look of someone who drank black coffee, read Greek for fun, and hadn't experienced doubt since 2002. He spoke confidently in English, with an accent, and a translator echoed him for the rest of the room. And just like that, the event was underway, miracles pending.
The program for the seminar was straightforward. First came the introduction to the Gospel; basic teachings about who Jesus is and what Christianity is all about, with of course, and extra-focus on the Book of Acts. Then came step two: the hands-on part. John was accompanied by a team, and they called this whole setup a "kickstart."

The idea was to not just *learn* about faith, but to *live* it, immediately. After the teaching, the staff would be available to pray with anyone who wanted to confess their sins, repent, and take the next steps. Those next steps? First, receiving the Holy Spirit, usually marked by ***speaking in tongues**.

And then, getting baptized in water. They even had an inflatable swimming pool ready to be set up the next morning, right there at the house, for Day Two of the seminar.

**To say strange words that no one can understand, especially as part of a religious experience.*

They were extremely charismatic, like, smiling-with-their-whole-face charismatic, and seemed genuinely full of love for humanity. They cared about their neighbour's fate in the afterlife as if it were their own... which, in hindsight, might explain why they had such urgency, like God had them on commission. And honestly? I was drawn to it. Deeply. How could I not be? After everything I'd been through, the rejection, the confusion, the years of spiritual whiplash; this felt like certainty wrapped in a warm hug. These people didn't just believe in God; they acted like they were on a first-name basis with Him. It was intense, yes, but also comforting in a strange way. They looked like they *belonged* somewhere. They had a mission. A purpose. A spiritual family. And I, well... I was just tired of floating.

Looking back now, it almost feels like the most predictable plot twist of my life. Of *course* I fell for it.
I was vulnerable, raw, still bleeding from wounds I didn't even know I had. It was a perfect storm: they were offering answers, belonging, healing, and I was craving all three like oxygen. So yes, it was bound to happen. Me, fresh out of religious exile, walking straight into a room full of miracle-chasing Christians with an inflatable baptism pool in the trunk. I mean... what could possibly go wrong?

–

Their message about confessing, repenting, turning away from your sins and never looking back, *that* part hit me the hardest. Not because it was new, but because it felt like a promise. Like I could wipe the slate clean. Erase everything. Be born again, not just spiritually, but emotionally, physically, psychologically.

And yes, that's what they preached. That's what God offers in the Bible. But I didn't want it to unfold slowly, over time, with patience and healing. I needed it right then. Immediately. Like a reset button. Like magic. And the way they spoke; so certain, so confident, it felt like they were holding a bottle labelled *"Start Over"* and offering it to me without even asking my name.

That night, alone in the guest room where I was staying, I took out a notebook. I sat on the bed, shaky, but hopeful and almost giddy, like a little girl about to be adopted by the perfect family she'd made up in her head. The utopian one. Then I started writing down all the sins I wanted to confess. Everything I wanted to be free from. Everything I wanted God to look at and say, 'Let's pretend that never happened.' But as I wrote, something strange happened. Some of the things on that list, things I called sins, weren't mine. They were things *done to me*. Things I'd survived. Things I'd absorbed so deeply, I had started to believe they were my fault. Like maybe, if I named them in ink and repented hard enough, I could be clean from the pain. Maybe I could be whole.

I didn't know it at the time, but I wasn't just repenting for my choices. I was apologizing for my pain. For my trauma, and for having survived in ways that weren't pretty or perfect or praise-worthy. I didn't see the difference yet. I just wanted it all gone.

–

My hosts were just as enthusiastic as I was, though they were already baptized and well along in their faith. They understood my excitement, maybe not the sheer intensity of it, but enough to smile knowingly, like people watching someone fall in love for the first time. So, when we returned the next day, I confessed my sins through tears. One by one, each person who had done the same stepped forward and went under the water, reborn. I found it beautiful, the idea that so many people could walk in heavy with demons and walk out dripping, shivering, and free. Or at least freer than they were ten minutes earlier. I wanted this, whatever this is. No, I needed it.

When I walked over to the swimming pool, I was nervously rubbing my hands, not because I was being filmed like some kind of spiritual circus act, but because I was surrounded by strangers who looked thrilled for me, and I didn't know them at all.
John was standing inside the pool, holding my right hand. On my left was a curly-haired woman I'd never seen before. And then, before I could even brace myself, John started shouting my sins out loud, for everyone to hear. I froze. I felt naked. There it was: my trauma, my past radicalization, my bondage, all blasted on loudspeaker. He kept shouting, promising that when I came out of the water, I'd be free. Free from all of it.
I didn't even have time to react before I was under. John pushed my head down, squeezing my hand, while the woman held on tight. Above the surface, it was a spectacle. Below the surface, it was something else entirely. The roughness of it; all the hands, the force, made my body remember things I hadn't consented to remembering at all. Suddenly, I was there again: my mother hitting me with a belt.

Brrr — the muffled rush of water in my ears.
Hah! Hah! Hah! — like the rhythm of a belt cracking against my back.
Huuuuh! — me gasping, lungs searching for air.

And somewhere in that blur, I wondered: Is this what deliverance feels like?
Or is it just trauma reenacted; another ritual dressed up as healing, trying to scare the demons out of me by dragging the past back in? And then, Brrr, again. 'You pig!' (in my mother's voice). Huuuuh! me surfacing, breathless, only to hear John screaming in tongues.

I remembered, under the pressure of the moment, that this was the part where I was supposed to speak in tongues too, that's what the others before me did. That's what happens now, right? If I didn't, I wasn't sure what they'd do. Maybe keep dunking me until I did. So, I did. Whispering through exhaustion, drenched in holy water, I said it: "Shambaradaraka..."

And just like that, everyone started to clap.

I couldn't cope with the attention. Everyone suddenly knew my story, and they flocked to me, beaming, saying how *blessed* I was to have found God. But the way I heard it was: "How blessed are you! Your situation was so hopeless, you were almost a lost cause but look what God did with *even* you! Isn't He amazing?"
What they meant as encouragement, I heard as spiritualized pity. Like I'd become a walking cautionary tale with a redemption arc stapled on. "Thank you for reminding me," they'd say, "that even though I haven't been through what you did, there's still hope for me."

That's what compliments become when you've never been safe, when your basic human needs have always been unmet. When you haven't known consistent food, protection, love, or dignity. They stop being compliments. They become a kind of performance review: evidence that your suffering has finally made you useful to someone else's faith.

They're not affirmations. They're appropriations. They say more about the speaker's relief than my healing, but they made me feel isolated inside, and why should I complain? At least now, my demons are gone. I should be grateful. I have a family now.

Christ said that we are a family in Him: *"Whoever does the will of my Father in heaven is my brother and sister and mother"* (Matthew 12:50). So now, I have everything I ever wanted. A family. A place to belong. I *should* be happy. But the word *should* carry weight I can't lift.
It suggests something is wrong with me if I'm not overflowing with joy, not fully basking in the miracle of being "found." And yet, even in this newfound family, I felt like a guest in someone else's home. Everyone was kind. Loving, even. But kindness isn't the same as safety. Kindness is a warm coat. Safety is knowing the storm's passed. And love, if you've only known it with conditions, feels more like a performance review than a promise. They told me I was finally home. But how do you feel at home when your body's still bracing for exile? When your nervous system still twitches like it's waiting for the door to slam, the faces to turn cold, the rules to shift without warning?

I wanted to belong. I tried to. But trying to feel safe isn't the same as being safe. And healing isn't a matter of theology, it's something that takes root slowly, in silence, in time, in places where no one is fucking clapping

Chapter 3

One day, honestly, I don't even remember where I was or what I was doing, John made me an offer.

"Come to the Pioneer Training School," he said. "At the Jesus Hotel."

The *Jesus Hotel.* I mean... are you kidding me? A hotel. For Jesus. How could I say no? There was just one small problem: I couldn't pay for any of it. Not the school, not the plane ticket to Aalborg, Denmark (where even *is* Denmark? Is that the place with windmills? Vikings? IKEA?). I still had the same suitcase I'd carried out of the airport months ago. Same clothes. Some of them hadn't been washed in longer than I'd like to admit. My whole life fit in a tiny, slightly sour-smelling bag.

But this? This was an opportunity. A chance to meet my new widespread Christian family, strangers who would love me because we shared the same Father: God. Turns out spiritual DNA is easier to claim than emotional responsibility.

That's the thing about Christian *love.*
It shows up fast.
Like a *bomb.*
Big, loud, and out of nowhere.

John ended up transferring me eight hundred euros to cover everything, flight, school, the works. Just like that. How freaking generous, I thought.
And then, there it was.

Tom, the founder of The Last Reformation himself, posted a video of my baptism. My story. Me. He spoke with passion, sharing how incredible it was that I was coming to the school. That God was moving powerfully through my life. And I watched, wide-eyed, as strangers online celebrated me.

Me.

A little wreck of a girl with one suitcase and barely clean clothes. A history so heavy I could barely carry it. My past was like that stubborn smell you try to wash off, but it clings, like cheap perfume gone wrong or a mystery stain on your favourite shirt. Suddenly, in the eyes of strangers, I was someone worth talking about.

It felt like being lifted into the sky, like I'd been plucked from the bottom of the ocean and tossed into a cloud of warm, fluffy affirmation. Loved. Not just accepted but celebrated. Seen. After a lifetime of being invisible, unless I was in trouble or some crisis blew up, I was now someone whose tears were holy, whose pain had purpose. Like a sacred art installation no one dared walk past without whispering, "How brave." But what they really meant was, *thank God it's not me.* That's the unspoken chorus behind every applause I got: a soft murmur of relieved spectatorship dressed up as inspiration.

They gave me in weeks what I'd craved my whole life: attention, care, softness. People held my gaze, really held it, like I wasn't some ticking time bomb or an inconvenient shadow to ignore. They asked questions, waited patiently for my answers, said I was precious. That I didn't have to earn love. Imagine that. Love, no strings attached. Wow. I didn't see the strings because they braided them into halos.

I believed them. Of course I did.

I was floating in this cloud, dizzy and high on kindness like a junkie who suddenly got a prescription.

But clouds don't last.

And what I didn't know, what no one ever warns you about, is that this kind of love... can disappear just as fast as it arrives. Like your favourite TV show getting cancelled after the first season.

This love wasn't just conditional; it was *hyper*-conditional. Love with a cliffhanger and fine print you only read when it's too late. At least my mom was loud; raw and brutal in her unpredictability. I could read the rhythm of her chaos, even if it hurt. There was a twisted kind of structure to her version of love. But with The Last Reformation? I had no map, no compass, no clue what to expect. The rules kept shifting, silently, but surely, and the love felt like it was always on the edge of vanishing. And when it left, it didn't just take the warmth; it rewrote the memory of ever having been held. It made you doubt whether comfort was something you earned or just hallucinated.

Sometimes, it leaves even faster.

Especially when you stop performing.

Especially when you start asking questions.

But I hadn't asked anything yet.

Not yet.

That came later.
After the Jesus Hotel.
After the school.
After I stopped being the miracle...

...and started being a problem

PART 7

THE QUIET GOODBYE

Chapter 1

What I didn't know then, and couldn't have understood, was how desperately fragile my mental health had become. It was like my brain had been living in a war zone, and no one told it the fighting was over. I was carrying the weight of years of trauma, but no one, including me, recognized the signs for what they really were. The abuse I endured as a child, both physical and emotional, had left invisible wounds I didn't yet understand. The fear that clung to me was a silent prisoner, shaping every breath without my awareness. Instead, everything I was experiencing got wrapped up in spiritual language: "spiritual attacks," "demonic oppression," "testing of faith." These terms became convenient language to describe what no one was trained to see: a mind and body overwhelmed by trauma, screaming for healing beyond prayer alone.

When my heart began to pound like it was trying to jailbreak through my ribs, and I gasped for air, the brown scarf returned; not physically, but in sensation. A phantom noose. Scratchy, invisible, and loyal as ever. Panic's favorite accessory never left the wardrobe of my mind.

I was told I was under attack from demons, or Satan. What it really was, though, was my body reacting to the constant flood of fear and stress I'd buried deep inside. My nervous system was still stuck in survival mode; reliving moments of terror I had no way to process.
Every breath was a negotiation.
Every silence felt rigged.
It was like my body had memorized fear in a language I didn't speak. Every creak in the floorboards became a prophecy.

There were times when a sudden touch or loud noise made me jump, my whole body freezing or flinching like I was reliving something awful. They called it weakness or a lack of spiritual strength, not enough faith. The control implemented in the sect was subtle and unsaid but deeply understood. There were unspoken rules, not written anywhere, but enforced through *social pressure* and *spiritual implication*.
No need for chains when the glances do the job.

Unspoken rule: You should not take your medication. If you need antidepressants or anxiety meds, it's because your faith isn't strong enough. Taking them meant you still depended on something human for the things God was supposed to heal in you. It meant admitting you were weak, and in this world, weakness equalled sin.

Unspoken rule: Don't question leadership. You could ask clarifying questions, but you could never challenge or disagree. Any discomfort you had with the teachings or practices was seen as rebellion or spiritual immaturity. Or as Tom often said: 'A stab in his back'. Even thinking critically felt dangerous.

Unspoken rule: Don't look too sad, too lost, too broken. Be visibly joyful, after all, the Holy Spirit brings peace. If you're crying too much or seem depressed, it casts doubt on your salvation. You start feeling like a liability to the movement instead of a testimony.

Unspoken rule: Don't form deep friendships outside the movement. If you're emotionally close to people who aren't "in the Spirit," you risk spiritual contamination. Even family becomes suspect. Isolation was disguised as holiness. Protection.

Unspoken rule: Don't rest. Time off means you're lukewarm. You're not praying enough, preaching enough, fasting enough. Exhaustion wasn't a red flag, it was a badge of honour, proof that you were "on fire for God."

These rules weren't written down. They didn't need to be. You absorbed them by watching who got praised and who got corrected, who was spotlighted and who was quietly pushed aside. But it was my body remembering the abuse, the nights I lay awake terrified of what might come next. It was my trauma screaming to be noticed. The leaders' words landed like blows, 'You just need more faith', they'd say, as if my struggles were a personal failing rather than the echoes of past horrors, but apparently, what I really needed wasn't therapy, it was jazz hands for Jesus.

It was my trauma screaming to be noticed. And yet, even in moments meant to symbolize peace and healing, that scream followed me, louder than ever. The worst was during that baptism, the moment John pushed my head under water roughly, squeezing my hand so tight I thought I might break. I was supposed to feel reborn and cleansed, but all I could feel was the past crashing in on me, the sting of a belt, the sharp words, the helplessness I felt as a child. The water around me wasn't holy; it was cold and suffocating. A trigger dragging me back into a place I had spent years trying to escape. I started to dissociate during those moments. My mind would go blank or drift far away, like I was no longer in my body. I felt like I was failing somehow, failing God, failing the community, failing myself. After that moment, I found it harder to reconcile my faith with my pain. How could God's cleansing feel like drowning? The difference between what was expected and what I felt widened into silence and confusion. My worth depended on others so much, I started to dissociate during those moments; my mind would go blank or drift far away, like I was no longer in my body. The leaders said I was resisting the Spirit or that I needed to "surrender" more fully. Their accusations felt like a slap in the face. I was drowning in fear and pain, but they told me it was my fault, that I wasn't holy enough. This made me shrink inward, feeling invisible yet exposed all at once. But what was really happening was my brain trying desperately to protect me from pain it couldn't face. Emotionally, this misunderstanding crushed me. I felt like I was failing somehow, failing God, failing the community, failing myself. I was told to pray harder, to have more faith, to push through. Instead, I felt more alone than ever. My trauma wasn't being seen or heard; it was being covered up with expectations and spiritual jargon that made me doubt my own experience. I remember once breaking down in tears during worship, hands trembling, chest heaving—and someone leaned in and whispered, 'Just give it to Jesus.' I wanted to scream. My trauma wasn't being seen or heard; it was being papered over with slogans and expectations.

I was trapped between my pain and the demand to be "whole" and "holy." To be 'holy' meant to wear my wounds like badges, but only in a way that served their image. Perfection wasn't about healing; it was about presentation. I learned to smile through tears, hiding the chaos beneath a mask of piety. It was a kind of spiritual isolation, being surrounded by people who loved me in theory but couldn't meet me where I was. And the more I tried to fit their expectations, the more lost and broken I felt inside. I was piecing myself together with spiritual duct tape. I started to feel less like a person and more like a marketing testimony.
My pain got a promotional thumbnail and a clickbait caption. My story wasn't mine anymore, it was used to promote The Last Reformation.

I remember the day my testimony was posted online; edited and polished to highlight only the 'miraculous' moments, stripping away the messy, painful parts. I was a product, not a person. And I wasn't the only one. Anyone with a "take-your-breath-away" story caught Tom's attention and got their own video on his page, spotlighting their struggle like a trophy.

Remember when I said I became a problem? That's because I'd never spoken these thoughts out loud before. I was always confused about Tom. Still is, sometimes. He seemed like this childlike, tall man, genuine, caring, almost like a father to me. So, who was I to criticize him? It felt like cursing a lifeboat for leaking after it saved you from drowning, but you're still wet, and now the boat's got a megaphone.
Who was I to spit in the water that was given to me when I was thirsty? But deep down, the water wasn't always clean. It poisoned me. Slowly, quietly, like a small parasite in my veins. And there's no way in hell I would

let anyone wander by, thirsty and hopeful, without warning them, just because I was confused.

My feelings are tangled, messy, like trying to hold onto soap in a storm. I was both grateful for the love I thought I found, the temporary shelter he provided, the food... and horrified by how it twisted me.
Back then, I couldn't put it into words. But now, looking back with clearer eyes, I see the machinery behind sects, how they wrap you in warmth, only to slowly tighten the noose. They use charm and belonging to draw you in, only to isolate you from the outside world, controlling every thought until your identity is theirs to mold. And the one thing that can truly set you free? Speaking up. No matter how many demons I "cast out," how many kickstarts I helped in, how many strangers I prayed for on cold snowy city streets until their tears mingled with mine, how many times I preached my lungs raw on benches in Aarhus, none of it was the glue holding me together. Even after I decided to leave, just before The Last Reformation was exposed by a national Danish TV channel, and Tom fled to Florida like a bad sequel, I kept sending him messages. Encouragement. Spiritual armour against what I thought were attacks from Satan. I held on to a sliver of hope that maybe, just maybe, things could be different if I kept fighting from the outside. Or perhaps I was afraid of fully letting go, not ready to face the void alone.

I didn't start criticizing when I left. I started questioning, doubting, unravelling the moment I met someone who didn't try to drown me in holy water, but instead, held up a mirror, a woman named Camilla Johnson.

She didn't offer me a stage, a slogan, or a scripture. She offered something far more dangerous: truth.

What she showed me didn't just shift my beliefs; it ruptured them, like someone unscrewing the lid on a jar you've been trying to pry open for years with bleeding hands. But that part — how she cracked the code and named what no one else dared to — is another chapter. One I wasn't ready to live, let alone tell. Not yet.

The reason I left wasn't some dramatic, Hollywood-style escape from a cult. It was a coincidence, almost accidental. One day, I was traveling to Tunisia with my friends Kim, who was the first I became my close with when I arrived at The Jesus Hotel and Helle.
On the way back from our missionary trip, instead of flying straight to Aalborg, we decided to land in Copenhagen. Kim had reached out to a friend, someone I'd met briefly before, who had also visited the Jesus Hotel. She was a friend of Helle's and kindly offered to let me stay in her apartment in Frederiksberg.

And just like that, I vanished — no announcement, no bang. Just the quiet exit of someone who'd finally learned not to wait for permission. No one from The Last Reformation asked where I'd gone. No one wondered why I never came back. It was as if my story, once a shining beacon fuelling their movement, had run out of fuel. The marketing value dried up, and suddenly, I became invisible, and that feeling, that sudden erasure, was startling. The same community that had showered me with love and attention, as if I was irreplaceable, simply forgot I existed when I stepped out of their line of sight.

The love bombing had been a lie and a performance. When I disappeared, so did the love.

When I settled in with Tara, I would later come to realize that Frederiksberg is like the Cannes of Copenhagen, quietly elegant, almost unreal in its calm and charm. I felt lucky to be living there, even if I hadn't quite earned it.

Tara was everything I needed without even trying. Warm, welcoming, with this innocent, effortless aura that made you feel safe just by being near her. Living with her was like stumbling into a parallel universe, one where women my age weren't spiritual mascots or trauma punchlines, but just... alive. Free to laugh, to sleep in, to exist without performance. She was funny and goofy in the best ways, and every time I started to open up, no matter how messy or broken the words were, she just listened. No advice, no rushing me to fix things or push past the pain, no Bible verses to end the conversation, she simply *was* there, with me, holding space for everything I couldn't say anywhere else.

But here's what no one tells you about cults: they ghost harder than Tinder dates.
One minute you're the chosen one, drenched in divine purpose. The next? You're just spiritual spam; from the dizzying highs of love and attention to the sudden, crushing void when you leave.
One day, you're the shining star, the "irreplaceable" miracle, the living proof of the movement's power. The next day? You're a ghost. Forgotten. Erased. That disappearance wasn't some heroic escape with dramatic confrontation or fanfare. It was almost banal, just silence where noise used to be. No calls, no messages, no "Where did you go?" Just the cold realization that the story, the version of me they wanted, was no longer useful.

I felt like I had slipped through the cracks of an invisible machine, discarded like a used tool. Part of me wanted to scream, "I'm still here!" but the other part, wounded and exhausted, just wanted to vanish completely.

But then, out of the blue, John messaged me once. Just one message.

He expressed concern about my salvation, worrying that I was drifting away, that I wasn't hanging out with the other Last Reformation people anymore.
He noticed I'd stopped posting about preaching, stopped sharing Bible verses. I had gone quiet, just like they had. That single message was a ghost note from a dying system; proof they still believed my silence was their liability, not my liberation, and expecting me to live up to the story they had created. It was as if my silence was a danger to their narrative, something to be corrected or reclaimed. But for me, that quiet was the beginning of reclaiming *myself*.

On that plane, heading to Copenhagen instead of Aalborg, I was filled with a strange mix of guilt, relief, and a deep, aching loneliness I hadn't known I carried. Leaving wasn't a glorious break; it was a quiet unravelling. I was terrified of what would come next, yet somehow, I was finally free to breathe.

For me, friendship was always an audition. No matter how raw or real it got, I was still half-waiting to be told I didn't make the final cut. Betrayal wasn't a shock, but a muscle memory. Every quiet disappearance of people who promised they'd stay, I continued trusting immediately, openly, relentlessly.

But beneath that trust lay a quiet shield I never fully

lowered, whispering confidently: "When they leave, it won't change anything. It'll just confirm what you've always known: that you aren't enough, not as a friend, not as family, not even as someone passing by."

It wasn't people I didn't trust. It was my ability to be lovable without being useful.

If a friendship ended, it stung, but I remained intact; you can't break what was never whole, but you can disturb the dust where something like a heart tried to grow.

Frederiksberg felt unreal, like I'd wandered into someone else's dream. Too calm. Too kind. Like waking up in silk sheets after years of sleeping on broken glass, unsure if softness was a trick. It was quiet. No one expecting me to be a miracle or a testimony.

Here, I could just be broken. And still be worthy of kindness. But receiving that kindness stirred a storm inside me.

I wasn't used to being seen without strings attached.

It felt foreign and frightening, like standing on the edge of a cliff, debating whether to leap into the unknown or climb back to safety, all while a bear thundered behind me.

Do I turn and fight, risking survival and scars, or do I jump, hoping the fall is less brutal than the bear's jaws?

My heart ached with the knowledge that pain, and loss could return at any moment, so I held my walls tight, even around her. But even as Tara's kindness surrounded me, wrapped around my brokenness like a soft blanket, I couldn't fully receive it in my heart.

I was prepared for that loneliness like a shadow waiting in the wings, lurking beneath every smile and gentle word. It was as if my heart was caught between wanting to trust, to believe that someone could really see me and stay, like the hard-wired fear that this too was temporary,

another illusion that would shatter.
I wasn't healed. Not yet. But at least, I was somewhere safer. The ghosts still followed me, but for once, no one asked me to silence them in exchange for love.
Tara never tried to fix me. She just made coffee and slid it across the table without asking why my hands were shaking. She didn't quote scripture or tell me to smile. She let me sit there, unravelled, hollowed out, and wholly human.

No spotlight. No performance. Just breath. Just room.

And maybe that's where healing begins; not with a miracle, not with some grand epiphany, but with someone saying nothing and staying anyway.

Chapter 2

At nineteen, the reality of Copenhagen hit me all at once. I was alone in a country with a language that sounded nothing like French or English, under skies so grey they felt personal, another enemy to add to my list, and I'd never lived somewhere where negative social control wasn't the main character. I'd never been responsible for rent, taxes, or even packing groceries "Tetris-style" into a bag to be more efficient. Is that a thing?
I hadn't learned these basic, banal life skills; not because I didn't care, but because my childhood was spent managing chaos, not preparing for adulthood. No one teaches you how to pack a grocery bag when every day feels like damage control.

Desperate for work, I landed a three-day trial at a café with no contract, no safety net, and was summarily fired for "reasons." Without a contract, I couldn't protest. Practically handicapped, I wandered those streets in distress, terrified that stability might undo me.
Then there was Tara's apartment: quiet, rent-free for a few months. I kept asking myself, *what did I do to deserve this?*
Later I'd learn that's just Tara's nature: generous, compassionate, endlessly giving. But at the time, opening my heart felt impossible.
Fear crept in.
Nightmares multiplied.
My anxiety soared.
I needed to feel like I belonged somewhere.

So, I started attending a new church in Copenhagen, let's call it Horizon Fellowship, because *"Welcome Home"* was written on every billboard in stark black and white on their building.

From the moment I stepped inside, it felt like being adopted by a perfectly choreographed society: welcome team, offerings team (the tithe collectors), worship team (the stage stars).
Strangers greeted me like long-lost royalty, eyes wide with genuine surprise that *I* hadn't known this place before.
Every Sunday, I found myself on the offerings team alongside my friend Kim, and sometimes Tara.
It was intoxicating. Finally, a place to process my trauma through laughter, songs, and "family".
Until, slowly, I wasn't interesting anymore.
The warm welcome cooled into routine hellos; the compliments dulled into polite nods.

And that's when my gut screamed: *This is love-bombing all over again.* I'd been here before, in another "reformation" that promised purpose but demanded my very self in return. Yet, stripped of tools or language to name my distrust, I stayed.
Fear whispered: *Without this community, where would you be?*

That's how it works; they drown you in affection like it's a holy hot tub. You barely have time to breathe before you're marinated in hugs, hallelujahs, and unsolicited life advice. But once you're "in," recruited in one of the teams, the warmth moves on.
They don't retire, they just redirect, love-bombing the next shiny newcomer while you're left in the background, holding a folding chair and wondering if we were all just puppets in matching t-shirts, calling it "serving" while handing out free labor like candy, each of us starving for affection, powering a megachurch worth hundreds of millions with nothing but our broken hearts and good intentions; and I watched it happen in real time, the same script played out on new faces, wide-eyed and grateful, still unaware they were next in line to be forgotten.
But eventually, I saw the outlines of control beneath the kindness. My heart learned to spot the forest through the trees of praise and platitudes. I realized I'd traded one sect for another — not a traditional cult, but a well-meaning community that still wasn't healthy for *me*. It wasn't that I expected constant adoration, or that I wanted to be endlessly love-bombed. I wasn't looking to be treated like a miracle; I just wanted to be treated like a person. What I craved was something steadier: connection without performance, community without compliance. I needed room to be quiet sometimes, to show up messy, confused, unsure. But there was no space

for ambivalence in a place that ran on certainty and spectacle.

You're either shining or slipping, either fully in or suspiciously out. And I wasn't either. I was human; and that, somehow, made me incompatible.

But here's the thing they don't put on the billboard: belonging without boundaries isn't safety. It's theatre. And churches, like families, can sometimes mistake intensity for intimacy.
What I didn't know then, and what no one teaches you when you're young and desperate for connection, is that **some communities don't love you; they love your compliance**.
They love your healing story, your attendance, your willingness to serve. But they don't love your doubts. Or your nos.
Or your opinions.
Or your questions that don't end in a Bible verse.

I wasn't taught that healthy community makes room for silence, for space, for you to say, "I'm not okay," without becoming a project.
Maybe that's the lesson: **Not every place that calls itself a home is built for your kind of healing.**
Some houses will just hurt you in softer tones. And when you're someone who grew up thinking pain was proof of love, that kind of hurt feels familiar, almost comforting. You don't even realize you're bleeding until you're asked to clap louder, smile wider, and "just trust the process".

And if you leave? Don't worry, they'll just "pray for you." Which, in church language, is passive-aggressive for "enjoy hell, sweetie."
If I had a krone for every time someone prayed for my lost soul, I could probably start my own mega-church,

but don't worry, it'd come with boundaries, trauma-informed communion, and a "skip worship if you're tired" policy. I don't know exactly when I stopped needing to be saved and started wanting to be seen. Maybe it was sometime between handing out offering buckets and googling "how to know if your church is a cult (but like, a cool one)".

But I do know this: I'm not here to preach. I'm here to piece together something human out of all the shattered bits. And if I seem a little awkward or intense while doing it, well, you know... at least I'm consistent.
Turns out, healing is less about having it all figured out, and more about still showing up, heart slightly limping, snack in hand, ready to try again.

I understood then that no matter how warm the welcome or glossy the gospel, true belonging can't be forced. Instead, it must grow from genuine soil, not pity, not praise, but truth.
And that soil? I'm learning to build it myself, on my own terms, with hands that finally know they're *mine.*

I did meet some amazing people at that church.
Some of them still walk beside me, still pick up the phone. They remind me that not everything born in a broken place is doomed.
But that church also gave me **him**, the pro football player with the Bible in one hand and a thousand unread messages in the other. Spiritually seasoned, or so it seemed. Charismatic, cocky, always framed by the kind of attention that made him both admired and misunderstood. People saw a career. I thought I saw a person. His attraction to me was... loud. The kind of compliments that were so kind they made me uneasy. But it was new, being seen that way. Desired.
He felt like safety with swag. His voice, his pauses, the

way he listened, it gave me the illusion that someone, finally, *got* me.

So, when we lay on a blanket under the stars, talking about home and loneliness, I believed him. I believed myself. We rode back to my place, me on the back of my own bike while he pedalled. I remember being surprised by his stamina, then laughing at myself; *of course* he was strong, he was a damn athlete. But I forgot. I'd already started reconstructing him in my mind, piece by piece, from shared silences and small smiles.
Not from his career, but from who I hoped he was.

At home, we poured wine, just a glass. Then two. I remember the way his eyes shifted, how he leaned in, got closer, and with a grin and asked, "Think you can down that in one go?" I didn't want to. But saying no felt like breaking something delicate.
So, I did. To be fun. To be light. To belong.
I didn't know what he wanted. Not really. But later, when his movements became sharper, faster, as if I were a problem to solve with force, when my body froze and I stopped trying to make sense of it, I realized I wasn't part of this. I was just something to get through.
And somewhere in the middle of it, his warm breath hit my ear, and he said, *"You should replace this fat with muscle."*
That was it. That's what my brain decided to keep.

The worst part?
I'm not even sure he knew what he was doing. Or if he realized. And that's the cruel thing about this kind of pain, there's no clear villain, no courtroom testimony, no dramatic confession. Just me, sitting in the silence that followed, wondering if I gave permission or just didn't resist hard enough.

Coercion doesn't always scream. Sometimes it smiles.

Sometimes it pours wine and compliments you into submission. And when it's over, you're left with the kind of doubt that burrows deep, because no one held you down, but you didn't walk in wanting this either.
It's a ghost of a wound. Hard to name. Harder to forget.
And in the end, it doesn't matter what he meant to do.
What matters is what it did to me.

The next morning, Tara went to work. I sat on the couch until she came back, biting my nails until they bled.
Not thinking or crying.
Just... paused.
As if breathing too loudly might summon whatever darkness was crouched in the corner, waiting to finish what he started.

At church, we orbited each other like strangers. Avoiding eye contact like it was contagious.

The pattern was familiar.
The intensity. The disappearance.
The switch from "special" to "nothing."

That night, I couldn't keep myself safe.
That night, I trusted someone who made me disappear.
And in doing so, I confirmed what I already feared: that to some people, I was only ever a moment.
A thing to pass through.
A body with a story, but not really worth reading twice.

The next morning, when I heard the turn of the key, Tara stepped in.
Her purse still dangled from her hand, the scent of wind clinging to her clothes. She hadn't even taken off her

shoes.
She looked at me.
I looked back.

And then I shattered.

The sobbing came from somewhere deep, somewhere I didn't know had sound.
She didn't ask what was wrong, she just sat down next to me and waited. And when I finally spoke, my voice cracked through the silence like a thin branch under weight.
I told her everything. Or at least, the pieces I could still reach.

She listened.
Like it mattered. Like *I* mattered.
For a moment, which was enough.

But a few days later, I went back to life as if nothing had happened. I folded clothes, answered messages, laughed at something dumb on my phone.
Because that's what I've always done; something breaks, and I keep moving. Because the alternative is too dangerous: to stop.
To feel.
To let it sink in.

And while I carried on, brushing my teeth, buying groceries, refilling the kettle, my brain stayed behind, staring at nothing.

At some point, I decided to speak up.
Not because I believed in justice, what would that even look like in a place where forgiveness replaced accountability? But because I was scared, he'd do it again.

To someone else.
Someone more vulnerable, with even less voice than I had.

Vulnerable?
As if I wasn't.
In my eyes, I was strong, resilient in the way survivors must be.
But strength doesn't cancel out fragility.
I was both.
Strong enough to speak.
Soft enough to still be bleeding.

So, I reached out to a female leader at the church. She invited me into a quiet office, just the two of us; two mugs on a coffee table between us, the air thick with sanctified tension.
I told her everything. Every halting word. Not as a shame-filled confession, but from a place of fear; the kind that coils around your gut when you realize silence might make you complicit. I wasn't looking for pity. I wasn't even sure I wanted comfort. I just knew that if I didn't say it now, it might happen again. And I'd carry that too.
You need to protect them, I told myself.
Just do it.

She listened.
Nodded.
And then said, gently, "I think it's best if you don't tell anyone else. Does this feel resolved for you?"

The room spun a little. I waited for the follow-up, some kind of reasoning, some protection, reassurance that he will be called in, something.

Instead, she placed her hand on mine and asked,
"Can I pray for you?"

Pray it quiet, in tongues;
as if syllables from heaven could mop up what a man's hands left behind.

She closed her eyes. I kept mine open.
Someone had to stay conscious.

I nodded, because what else do you do when your pain gets spiritualized into something private, polite, and profoundly lonely? She prayed, and I wondered if God was listening — or if even He had left the room.
My confession stayed there, in silence, in the air, in the moment his breath touched my ear, and his words carved something cruel into my body: *You should replace this fat with muscle.*
And I didn't tell many people afterward, not because I didn't want to, but because the words sounded absurd out loud. *He told me to replace fat with muscle.* And somehow, that gutted me more than his hands ever did. There are sentences that don't haunt you, they *inhabit* you, like rust in the walls of your own body. I didn't know it then, but his voice would echo in places hunger couldn't reach. And that was the last moment food ever felt innocent.

Chapter 3

The thing about this spiral is that you rarely notice when the floor disappears beneath you. It begins slowly, with a

few cancelled plans, unanswered texts, the quiet rationalizations: you're tired, overwhelmed, just need a night to reset.
You buy food you have no intention of eating, only to throw it out minutes later, as if testing whether your power still lies in refusal. And when someone asks how you are, you answer with that default grin, the one that dares them to ask again and begs them not to in the same breath. If they do, your whole body revolts, unsure whether it wants to confess, collapse, or snap.
It wasn't just food that lost its innocence, it was everything.

Rooms became places I drifted through without purpose, conversations blurred into white noise, and I'd find myself nodding, responding just enough to pass as present, though my body felt abandoned, like I was floating somewhere cold.
At night, I'd lie still, staring at the ceiling like it owed me answers. I'd whisper my name just to hear if it still sounded like someone worth keeping.
Sometimes it did, but most times, it didn't.

I didn't want to die — not exactly. I just didn't want to be here anymore. There's a difference, you know, but it's a quiet one, and it lives in the pause between decisions: one skipped meeting, one unanswered message, one day where you don't brush your teeth because what's the point? And no, it wasn't sad that I wanted to die.
I didn't cry when I thought about it.
I thought anyone would understand, if they really knew. It was like putting down a dog that's been hit by a car and can't be saved. You don't do it because you hate it. You do it because keeping it alive would be cruel. That's how it felt.
My disappearance wouldn't have been a tragedy; it would've been the kindest thing that ever happened to

me. At least to me.
You start wondering if disappearing could be gentle; like fading from the background of someone's memory, like fog slipping through a half-closed window. Which doesn't seem tragic, or messy, just... gone.

But then Kim would send me a voice note, completely unhinged and full of goofy nonsense, and I'd find myself laughing; the kind of laugh that startles you, because it's been so long that it scrapes your throat and leaves a breath of relief on the way out.
And in those moments, something held me in place, anchored me.
I stayed for them at first.
Eventually, sometimes, I stayed for me too.
Coping, if you could call it that, became a rhythm I stumbled through.

I went to church just enough to keep a sense of structure and partied just enough to erase it. Alcohol blurred the sharp edges, and attention became a sort of placeholder for intimacy, not quite love, not quite empty either. I danced like I was trying to shake grief out of my skin, let people touch me like I was transparent, as if the right person might see through me and name whatever was wrong.
And maybe I wanted that; to be seen so clearly that someone else could do the work of understanding me, since I had long given up trying.
Because when you're too tired to decipher yourself, the deepest hope is that someone else might look closely enough to translate you back to life.

But instead, I found myself staring at absence in the shape of a person.

Losing my mother while she was still alive was a grief I had no vocabulary for. She kept existing, baking like sugar could undo bitterness, but she didn't belong to me anymore. Or maybe she never did.

Grieving someone who lives is disorienting.

I tried talking to God about it, but after The Last Reformation, He and I had grown distant. We weren't speaking regularly, and it felt like He seemed more interested in me giving up sugar than giving up self-hatred.
I needed answers about why trauma shapes you like smoke, slipping through your fingers even when you name it, but He offered rules, silence, and repentance. The Jesus I followed back then, was a more celestial landlord than Savior, someone I tried to impress with fasting, modesty, and self-denial. I thought my emptiness was spiritual, I thought hunger meant holiness.
What it really meant was that I was very, very lonely.
I had simply traded one form of control for another, and the costume changed, but the role stayed the same.
So no, that wasn't healing, it was just adjusting the lighting, laughing louder than necessary, and posting golden-hour selfies like proof of life. Healing, back then, was a performance; one I directed, starred in, and sat through with clenched teeth, hoping no one would notice the cracks in the set.
On the outside, I looked better.
Better meant I ate sometimes.
Better meant I didn't pass out.
Better meant I smiled when people were watching.

And they clapped.
They clapped for the version of me that came back to life just enough to blend in.
And God help me; I couldn't bear to be seen, even as some part of me was silently begging to be held and not forgotten.

But breaking is quiet, punctual. And it always shows up wearing your own face, right?

It waits in the quiet, patient as dusk, like a current beneath still water.
By the time you feel the pull,
you've already let go of the oars,
already drifted too far from shore to scream for help.
You vanish into the tide without even knowing you'd begun to float.
No compass or anchor, just the memory of waves that once felt like home.

PART 8

LESS OF ME, MORE OF HER

Chapter 1

I didn't start with the goal of disappearing. Not consciously. I thought I was just taking charge. Long before gym memberships and calorie counters, there were dinner tables and isolating silences.
After his comment: *replace this fat with muscle*, something shifted. I wouldn't call it motivation; it was more like obedience. A quiet, compulsive urge to become what I thought he, and maybe the world, would finally approve of.

I joined a boxing gym like I was enlisting in a war I didn't know I was already losing. Four times a week, two-hour sessions, sweat, blisters, the occasional nausea. There was even a bin in the corner labelled "FOR VOMIT ONLY," as if that were a normal thing, like a friendly suggestion: "Throw up here, champ!"
It felt powerful, at least inside the gym. But power can be deceptive when it's built on fear. I didn't want to be strong; I wanted to be untouchable. Unbreakable. And being unbreakable looked a lot like disappearing.
When I got home, I ate nothing. Strong on the outside,

starving on the inside. I called it discipline, but I hadn't yet learned what it really was. It kind of wore a suit and tie, spoke in "health goals," but held a whip behind its back. At first, it felt like I was becoming someone better. Like I'd finally found the instruction manual for how to earn peace. And the first rule? Don't eat it.
The numbers were dropping.
The compliments were starting.
Especially from people who had no idea they were encouraging a slow death with a thumbs up. No one meant harm, but when shrinking earns applause, you stop questioning whether applause should ever come with suffering.
I felt like I had cracked some ancient code:
If you can't be safe, be smaller.
If you can't be loved, be impressive.
If you can't be understood, be less.
It was simple.
Brutal.
Addictive.

That revelation came later, much later.

Before calorie apps and gym passes, before shrinking felt like salvation, there was just a mirror.
And a classroom full of laughter.

It didn't feel like I was hurting myself. It felt like I'd finally found the emergency exit from failure.
And that voice... the voice inside me, the one that encouraged me with every skipped meal...

But long before hunger became my love language, there was another voice, real, loud, impossible to ignore: my mother's. My mother didn't whisper encouragement; she barked expectations. Her voice didn't wrap me in comfort; it wrapped me in pressure.

I didn't feel supported. I felt watched.
And in our house, being thin wasn't about health or happiness, it was about safety, control, competence and earning a temporary ceasefire in a war I never declared. A kind of approval that was rare in my house.
In our house, we weighed more than flesh, it was a thermostat for tension. So, I focused on the one thing I *could* manage: how I looked.
I couldn't change who I was; there was never enough room for her anyway. But I could shrink. I could control. I could become someone small enough to pass through the cracks unnoticed, to fold into corners, to avoid becoming a target.

And strangely, the only time my mother ever looked genuinely afraid of me was when I refused to eat. Not when I wept. Not when I screamed. Not when I shut down so completely that my silence filled the room. But when I pushed the food away, her posture changed.

She started walking carefully, as if every floorboard might set something off. She lowered her voice, left the door ajar, gave me space. And in that space — so, so rare in our house — it felt like I had finally done something right.

I didn't yet understand what was happening, only that emptiness seemed to earn me a kind of peace I couldn't access any other way; the chaos slowed, the volume dropped, and the girl who took up less space seemed to deserve more care.

That's how it begins. Not with mirrors or numbers or diets, but with a child discovering that withholding food is the only language anyone listens to.

The mother in my head didn't scream or sigh or disappear behind a slammed door. She didn't forget me. She appeared like clockwork when I skipped a meal, praised my discipline, wrapped her approval in hunger. Her love language wasn't words, it was absence.
Not the kind that leaves the room, the kind that leaves the plate empty and calls it care. I made her up, but she felt more loving, caring and real, than the one I had. This version of her loved me, so long as I obeyed.
She didn't snap, or sigh, or vanish behind the weight of her own exhaustion.
She watched. She noticed. She approved.
Every time I skipped a meal, she drew closer. Every hunger strike felt like her arms around me. Tight. Proud. Conditional.
The emptier I got, the more I felt held.

The scale was just a scoreboard. What I really wanted was applause. And the mirror at the gym didn't reflect progress — no, it reflected penance. Each bead of sweat was a confession. Each flex, a plea: *Do I look okay now? Am I enough?*
I needed applause, preferably not the slow kind they give at poetry readings. I wanted Olympic-gold, ugly-crying-on-the-podium applause.
But an app notification while wiping vomit off the bathroom floor?
Well, that was close enough.
This kind of applause: silent, digital, sterile. Just like the kind of love I thought I deserved, plus a medal.
Maybe just a break from hating myself.
Finally being seen.
Finally being safe.

And that's what made it so confusing. I didn't feel like I was hurting myself. I felt like I was succeeding, taking care of.

But looking back, I can see it clearly. I was building a cage. Not out of metal bars, but out of rules, routines, and praise, while telling myself I was winning. But I wasn't holding the reins, I was holding a stopwatch, a food scale, and my breath.
Shrinking to feel *held.*
Disappearing to be *noticed.*
Starving to feel *loved.*

And the cruellest part? That voice that made me feel safe was slowly, quietly, starving me.
Starving me from feeling, but I looked good.
From thinking, but I felt in control.
From rest, but I felt accomplished.
From connection, but I felt proud.

My mother made me feel the opposite.
She didn't starve me — she overwhelmed me.
With noise. With chaos. With expectations I could never name, let alone meet.

She didn't *leave space* for my feelings.
If I cried, I was dramatic. If I stayed quiet, I was cold and neglecting her.
So, I learned to starve my feelings, because being empty was easier than being wrong.

She didn't want me to *think for myself.*
She wanted obedience, silence, a daughter that didn't take up space.
So, I starved my thoughts, I let the voice inside take over, because it didn't argue or belittle.

She didn't *let me rest.*
Every moment was measured in productivity, in her exhaustion, in guilt.

So I starved my need for rest, I kept going until dizziness felt like achievement.

She didn't *nurture connection.*
Love was conditional, tied to appearances, weight, the shape of my body, how compliant I was.
So I starved my relationships, because the voice in my head at least told me "Good girl" when I obeyed.

My mother didn't say "I love you."
She said, "Eat!" or would not call me to eat.
She didn't say, "I'm proud of you." Because apparently, shame could be solved with carbs, and only if it was her idea.
She said, "You look sick. Eat", like my weight was a faulty thermostat she could reset with rice.

She adjusted my meals for her comfort — less food when I gained, more food when I lost.
And eventually, I internalized the lesson:
If I couldn't manage who I was, I could at least manage how I looked.
If I couldn't be lovable, I could be smaller.
Maybe if I took up less space, the world would have more room for me. Maybe if I became small enough, I'd finally fit inside someone's care.

Years before the app became my best friend and my judge, there was the voice — the one I thought was helpful.

The eating disorder wasn't a monster.
It was a translator.

It decoded a language I had been taught all my life:
Shrink, and you'll be safe.
Disappear, and you'll be loved.
Obey, and maybe, just maybe, someone will stay.

It was like living with a velvet-gloved captor: gentle enough to soothe me, firm enough to keep me obedient. The more I listened, the more I lost, weight, warmth, and eventually, clarity.
But the fewer the calories, the louder the praise.
The deeper the hunger, the deeper the comfort it gave me.
So I kept going.

I convinced myself that eating after a workout would cancel out the effort. That hunger meant results.

The gym itself was intense, it's the kind of place where pushing yourself too hard wasn't a red flag, it was a badge of honour. Honestly, I should've known then. Any gym where the puke bin is a regular feature should probably hand out therapy vouchers along with your membership card. Or at least a complimentary session with a nutritionist who doesn't think electrolyte imbalance builds character.
But I was too busy trying to become my final form: desirable, digestible, and conveniently silent.
Like I would finally become someone who could survive in a world where effort equalled worth.
Long before anyone praised me for shrinking, someone had already taught me I was too much.

But that belief didn't start there.

Of course, it began at home, in the shape of skipped meals, not as rebellion, but as a form of self-protection.

The dinner table wasn't a place to eat. It was a battlefield with side dishes.
Food wasn't comfort; it was chaos, arguments, tension, unpredictable moods.
Choosing not to eat and going to my bedroom instead, felt safer. Quieter. Being invisible was better than being a target.
But the dinner table wasn't the only place I learned to be ashamed of my body.
Long before I was counting calories or skipping dinner on purpose, shame had already laid its groundwork.

Like in middle school, when humiliation was fashionable... when one of the popular girls; loud, confident, and apparently fluent in humiliation, announced to the entire class that I had a "huge fat ass."
Just like that. No warning. No reason. Just a sentence thrown into the air like a joke, and the room lit up with laughter. Not the kind you join in on, but the kind that etches itself into your skin.
I remember feeling the heat rise in my face, but more than that, I remember the confusion. I hadn't really thought about my body before that. Suddenly, I was supposed to. Was I big? Had I always been? Why hadn't anyone told me? Or had they, in other ways?

From that day forward, I started examining my behind like a riddle I needed to solve. Some mornings, I'd feel enormous, like my body entered the room before I did.
It was like the mirror changed overnight.
One day, it stretched me into something grotesque; the next, I nearly disappeared. But no matter how long I stared, I never saw the same girl twice.
Other days, I felt small, almost translucent, like I could disappear if I tried hard enough.

It was like I'd been handed a pair of distorted glasses that no one else could see, but I couldn't take them off.

My body stopped feeling like mine. It became a performance I couldn't perfect. A thing people had opinions about. A shape to be assessed. And when the comments turned kinder years later, when people started complimenting me, they didn't feel like praise. They felt like puzzles I didn't know how to solve.
Was I thin enough now to be worthy of admiration? Or was I approaching some invisible line where concern would kick in?

There was never a clear answer, and maybe that was the most destabilizing part. So, I tried to fix it. All of it. The confusion, the fear, the shame. I did what I knew: I made a plan, followed rules, replaced food with discipline and emotion with control. I taught myself to stay ahead of the humiliation by becoming my own harshest critic. Because if I could master the script, if I could stay small enough, quiet enough, thin enough, maybe I could finally stop being the joke.
And my mother, consciously or not, reinforced it.
In her eyes, being "svelte*" was something to be glorified, not just admired, but *managed.* Comments made in passing, like a coach adjusting tactics mid-season.
If I lost weight, she seemed relieved. Proud, even.
But not too much, *then* I would "look sick, eat more", she would say.
So... what was I supposed to look like?
Too little, and she'd mutter that I looked sick, then toss my body into her catalogue of insults, like a faulty product she'd reluctantly keep the receipt for.
The praise was never just praise, it came barbed, like a compliment with a blade tucked inside. So, when control and praise started mixing in my adult life, I did not question it. I knew the rules. Thin was safe. Thin was

worthy.

svelte: attractively thin, graceful,* ***and* *stylish*

What started as obedience, gym, water, sleep, soon became devotion. Then fixation.
I wasn't just following rules; I was inventing new ones.
Rules like: water counts as food if it fills you up. Coffee is a meal. Hunger is progressing. I was both priest and sacrifice, kneeling at an altar of control with nothing left to offer but myself.

Every fast was a prayer I didn't dare speak.
Every hunger pang, a psalm of desperation.

Fast-forward to adulthood, where hunger came with algorithms and "wellness" felt a lot like quiet self-harm.
And because I searched for gyms, social media started feeding me ads for weight-loss apps...
Calorie counters. Macro trackers. Tools to "take control of your health." It didn't feel dangerous, not yet. It felt smart. Efficient. Adult.
I downloaded one of the apps, and it let me track my meals down to the gram, showed colourful graphs of progress, and even gave me gentle encouragements like "You are under your calorie goal today! Excellent job!"

Under. Always under. That became the goal.
Not "healthy." Not "strong." Just: *less.*

To measure my "progress," I bought a weight scale. Every morning, before drinking water or putting on socks, I stepped on it.
A new ritual.
A new number.
A new chance to prove I was succeeding.

Looking back, I wasn't tracking calories, I was measuring my worth in numbers that only went down. And the mirror, by then, had become a liar I trusted.
It told me I was almost there, almost small enough, good enough, gone enough.
And I believed it.
Every. Damn. Time.

Every app notification felt like applause, and every dip on the scale, like a standing ovation. I didn't realize I was becoming fluent in a new language, one where shrinking was praised, and silence meant success.
You know it's bad when your calorie app is the most supportive relationship in your life. It checked in on me more than my mom did. But at least it noticed when I was "doing well."
It sent me encouraging notifications like: "Excellent job staying under your goal!" as if it had any idea what I was losing beyond weight.
Spoiler: It wasn't just pounds. It was joy. Sanity. Myself.
And still, I clapped back, "Thanks, bestie."

From the outside, it looked like willpower. But inside, I was unravelling. The voice that once comforted me started sounding like a warden. And I began to wonder, what if this wasn't healing? What if I'd built a home inside the very thing that was hurting me? That's the trick of it. You think you're the architect of your recovery, then one day, you realize, you've just been decorating your own cage... throw pillows, scented candles, and just enough self-discipline to pass as healed, until you can't tell if you've built a sanctuary... or a tomb.

Chapter 2

On paper, things looked fine. I went to church every Sunday. I had a "connect group", which was basically Christian small talk with snacks.
I juggled part-time jobs, babysitting for French-speaking families, pulling espresso shots in cafes, waiting tables with forced smiles and aching feet. I had a room to sleep in, friends to laugh with, a God I thought I could count on. What else could I ask for?

From the outside, I looked stable. Responsible, even. To myself, it seemed like I was doing well. Eating less didn't set off alarms. It felt like proof, like I was finally adulting right. No more meltdowns, no public panic, just quiet, controlled effort. I had a job. I had a routine. And when you've been raised in a wildfire, even a quiet room that smells like smoke feels safe.

But looking back, I can see it for what it really was: a perfectly decorated illusion. A performance, not a life. I was succeeding at keeping the outside neat so that no one would look too closely at the inside. The cage was already there; I just hadn't named it yet.

And then she called.

My mother. Out of nowhere, like a ghost who only haunts when you've just started sleeping peacefully again. I don't even remember what I was doing when the phone rang. Something painfully normal, folding laundry, scrolling through a to-do list, sipping lukewarm coffee that tasted like performance.
Yeah, even my coffee had imposter syndrome.
And she didn't ask how I was doing. She didn't say she missed me. She started bashing me. For leaving. For abandoning the family. For "turning my back on everything we gave you."
"You think you're better than us now? Living like the French, huh?!" she snaps, her voice traveling through the phone like it was wired straight to her rage.
My passport might as well have been a declaration of war.

It wasn't a conversation, but a verbal autopsy, and I was both the corpse and the prime suspect. And just like that, the illusion cracked, and the control I thought I had unravelled like a thread pulled too hard.
My hunger had a new ache in it now; one I couldn't count in calories or log in an app. She didn't just reopen the wound; she excavated it, like a surgeon with a grudge and a God complex. After all, hadn't I asked for this? Wasn't this the price of growing up wrong? It was like she needed to remind me that no matter how much distance I built, she could still rearrange my insides with a single sentence. She didn't need to be in the room to reset the script, I was still cast as the villain in her gospel of sacrifice.
Her voice reached through the phone like it always had, snapping me back into that invisible daughter she'd designed. The obedient one. The grateful one. The one who didn't leave.

I could've been preaching the sermon or cleaning toilets for God's glory; it wouldn't have mattered. In her eyes, I was still the kid with too many feelings and not enough obedience.

My throat tightened. Not just from the words, but from the memories of every time I'd tried to explain myself and failed. Every time I had been told I was dramatic, ungrateful, disobedient. Every time I had to defend my right to exist differently than she wanted me to.

I hung up. I don't even remember how the call ended, only that the silence afterward was so loud it felt like someone had turned up the gravity in the room.

Even the air felt like it had something to say about my attitude.

And then I went to church. Because that's what I did. That was the life I had built: clean, composed, repentant. The Holy Trinity of self-denial.

I stood in worship with my hands raised and stomach empty, trying to believe that if I could just be good enough, faithful enough, small enough, God would take the rest away. Like some divine cashback scheme: suffer quietly, and maybe heaven sends a refund in joy. I tithed pain and waited for grace like it was backordered. Surely that's how it worked, right?

I was still counting calories, still skipping meals, still shrinking, but I was also praying, singing, and serving in the tithing team, with a smile.

I smiled when someone said I looked great, because apparently thin equals thriving. I nodded when the pastor talked about freedom in Christ, all while choking on my own ribcage.

That's the thing about high-functioning pain: it hides behind jobs and color-coded calendars. It's not fake. It's just a polished pain with a productivity filter. I wasn't

pretending. I just didn't know I was drowning.
Because when you grow up in chaos, stillness doesn't feel like peace, it feels like a setup. And when you finally get control over something, like your job, your meals, your shrinking body, you write the label "growth" on it and hope no one notices the rot underneath.
I wasn't healed. I was holy on the outside and haunted on the inside, and I wasn't talking about it, of course. Not out loud.
Why would I? What was I supposed to say: "Hey, I'm starving myself because it feels safer than receiving love?", God, no. I didn't speak 'feelings' yet. And even if I did, this kind of illness thrives in secret. Besides, what would church people do? Lay hands on me until I craved dinner?
Church people mean well, but fake pity is its own kind of violence. The kind that smiles while it backs away slowly, with the "I'll pray for you" kind of pity. The spiritual equivalent of ghosting.

So, I kept quiet. Polite. Productive.

And then I went back. Denmark to Cannes, France.
Still trying, because maybe if I moved back, I could fix it.

After all, I had learned so much since I left. Maybe I could explain it all better now. Maybe if I held eye contact long enough, they'd see a daughter instead of a defector. Maybe I could get my mom to feel loved, truly loved.
Even if she hurled every Arabic insult in the book at me five minutes later, maybe this time I wouldn't take the bait. Not because I didn't understand, God, I understood, but because I'd finally learned how to stay standing while it rained fire.
On most days, anyway.

This time, I'd had almost two years away from her. Two whole years to grow a spine or at least stitch one together from therapy quotes and quiet mornings. Maybe now I could face her without exploding or crying. Just survive proximity without bleeding.
I wasn't there to win. I just wanted the war to stop echoing in my chest every time she said my name.
I wanted to be able to breathe through a conversation without my body sounding the internal fire alarm.

My mom's favourite insult is practically a performance piece. When you pronounce it, it flows and when you scream it, it floods.
Loosely translated: "I curse your birth and the father who raised you, that filthy dog-pig."
Now that I think about it, she's always been a virtuoso of verbal assault. A true artist of offense.
Half the time, she wasn't just cursing *me*; she'd loop in our whole family, and occasionally herself for flair.
It was like emotional jazz: unpredictable, chaotic, and somehow still on beat. No one, not even her, knew where the next blow would land.

One minute it's my father, the next it's her own uterus for producing such ungrateful children. I used to flinch. Now I just wonder if she's ever considered stand-up. But this wasn't just about her.
Not entirely. That would be too easy.

It was about this aching belief that if I could just re-enter the story the right way, with no tantrum, no silence, no sarcasm, maybe I could rewrite the ending. Maybe I wouldn't be the villain anymore, and most of all, maybe I could see my sister and explain things the way I never could when it counted. Maybe I could say the words without flinching, this time. I packed my bags like I was trying to prove a theory — that love could be earned backwards, if you just showed up the *right* way.

Before I left, I had just started to feel like I belonged somewhere, with people like Tara, Kim, and of course, Sarah.

Sarah and I still argue about how we met.
I remember Monday football, when she was already laughing before the game started, moving like she was on fast-forward while the rest of us were buffering.
I leaned toward someone and whispered, "I want to be her friend," like I was placing an order.

She insists we met at church.

But I don't remember when we became friends, only that one minute we weren't, and the next, we were.
No buildup and no icebreaking, just two extroverts with matching damage and no volume control. It was the kind of friendship that made Denmark feel survivable, and maybe that's why I had to leave.
I needed more than survival, and I was ready to do anything to get there.

So I went back to France, thinking maybe this time, I could do it right. I didn't know it yet, but something was waiting for me there. Not comfort, or closure.
Just a quieter kind of damage — one that wouldn't show up in bruises.

PART 9

A LONELY HIGH

Chapter 1

After the going-away party with my church friends, I boarded a flight to Cannes, my childhood city.
Same sea. New me. But new doesn't always mean better. Sometimes it just means unrecognizable.
I thought I was stepping into a softer chapter, but all I'd done was wrap the silence in sunscreen and carry it to a different shore. I had found a one-room apartment across from the Catholic church I first stepped into since I converted. A full circle, or maybe just a spiral that learned to stand upright. It was small, but it had a view of something holy, which felt like a good omen. Or a warning. Hard to tell.

The beach was a five-minute walk away, so was my new job — bartender at a five-star hotel. I figured proximity to both heaven and hell might balance me out. The hotel had marble floors, guests who didn't smile, and bathrooms bigger than my entire apartment, with a presidential suite and butlers running everywhere.

On the plane, I felt strange. Free, but also... like someone had cut the strings off a marionette and said, "go be real."

Like someone had unbuckled the rules and told me I could do *anything* now.
Eat at a restaurant — just because.
Stay in, or out.
Dance until sunrise.
Go to a church, or don't.
No one would ask where I was.
No one would care.

It should have felt like liberation. Instead, it felt like a quiz I hadn't studied for. I didn't know anyone in Cannes anymore. Sanna had been sent to a Quranic school before we even made it to high school. Nadia? Vanished. Probably married. Or gone. Or working at Sephora. Who knows.

It was a fresh start, technically. But walking those streets felt like stepping back into a memory that had already made up its mind about me. Back then, I was *that* girl; the Muslim who became Christian. Basically, a local scandal with a pulse.
People didn't remember my name. They remembered the switch and it stuck to my face like a birthmark —proof that I'd done something unforgivable. Or worse: embarrassing.

I never liked Cannes.

People hear *Cannes* and think film festival, designer heels sinking into the red carpet and champagne that costs more than three-months rent.
The beach, the palm trees, the soft-focus glow of old money and new lips.

That part — the beach — I'll admit, I still loved.
The sea was the only honest thing in the city.

It didn't care who you were trying to impress or what label you wore, it just kept crashing in and pulling back, like clockwork with better posture.
But everything else felt like a stage play written by narcissists.
The city wore glamour like a prosthetic; polished, flashy, but stiff at the joints. You had to squint to spot the infection underneath: the quiet rot of people trying too hard to matter, to win, to sparkle just a bit brighter than whoever stood next to them.
Conversations felt like job interviews where the position didn't exist. Everyone smiled like they were auditioning for a toothpaste ad, but their eyes said they hadn't slept in years, probably because they were too busy checking if someone prettier walked into the room.

Cannes was the kind of place where having feelings was seen as an inconvenience, and growing up, I always felt like I was too much — too thoughtful, too intense, too sincere. Like I'd missed the memo that said: "Please keep your soul zipped up and your ambitions shiny."

I went to work every day like it was a performance, where you get ready, take the bus, change into the stiff hotel uniform, get semi-harassed by old Saudi royalty who technically owned twenty percent of the building and at least forty percent of the staff's dignity.
Keep your boundaries, but not too much.
You shouldn't make them unhappy.
Good thing I'd been trained to shrink and smile since childhood. I didn't need new skills. I'd been practicing those since birth: compress, comply, disappear attractively. But what could you expect from men who treated their Filipino staff like background music — always playing, never noticed — and still had the nerve to call them *Personal Assistants*, like the word "assistant" cancelled out the chains?

So, one flirt here, a Russian slap on the ass there, and voilà: hospitality! The industry where "the customer is always right" becomes a euphemism for "your boundaries are optional."

One morning, waiting at the bus stop, I saw someone I hadn't seen since middle school: Mila, a childhood friend.
"Hey! Mila? Wow, I almost didn't recognize you." I said surprised.
"Luna?! No way!" she said, just as shocked.

We caught up for a minute, exchanged contacts, and kept in touch from there. She looked as beautiful as ever, but what surprised me was how quickly she seemed to look up to me. I didn't really understand it — back in school, it had always been the other way around. I was the one who admired girls who acted like they had it all figured out. The ones who didn't flinch before raising their hand. The ones who walked like they knew where they were going.

This time, I'd left Copenhagen with freedom in my hands, and silence in my pockets. No friends. No fellowship. Just me and the city I used to call home, though it never quite returned the affection.
In Copenhagen, I had Helle to go out with. In Cannes, I had a good pair of running shoes. I'd run 10 kilometres just to feel like I existed. Sometimes I'd get recognized from my earlier presence on social media, my face jogging past strangers who used to double-tap it. The attention felt distant, like someone waving to a ghost.

What scared me wasn't being alone. It was bumping into someone who still remembered who I was *before*. The Muslim girl. The scandal. The conversion. My old life lived in whispers on these streets, and even though I'd changed, I wasn't sure I was allowed to be unrecognizable.

The job at the five-star hotel sounded impressive —until you remembered it came with rich men, invisible chains, and a uniform that felt more like camouflage than clothing. Everything gleamed, guests' jewellery, the suffocating weight of wealth. I brought drinks to women with fifty dresses hanging in their room, like they were planning to live several lives in one weekend. I thought of my mother's debts, her borrowed elegance, the performance of class we'd always failed to perfect. And then I pressed the elevator button with a professional smile.

Room 356. I remember that one. VIP floor. Man in his sixties, Saudi, eyes that undressed me before the door even clicked shut. He asked me where I was from — in Arabic. Probably saw the tattoo written in arabic on my collarbone. "Tunisia," I replied, still smiling. Hospitality, after all. He motioned for me to sit beside him. "You're very beautiful," he said. "Come."

I declined politely. Stepped toward the door. My stomach, however, stayed in the couch cushion. Then he reached for his pants. My heart stopped. But it wasn't a belt he grabbed, it was a 50-euro bill.
"Take it," he said.
I'd accepted tips before, but this one felt like it came with a receipt for my soul. I walked out feeling like I'd left something behind — something he didn't pay for but took anyway.

I ran every night after work. Didn't eat dinner. Just slept the hunger off. If I woke up lighter, quieter, maybe the

world would leave me alone.
Or at least look past me.

Mila texted me a few days after we reconnected at the bus stop. We'd started catching up like no time had passed, yes, except it had, and we weren't those girls anymore.
When she invited me to a party in the centre of Cannes, I said yes before thinking. I wanted to *belong*. Somewhere. Anywhere.

The parties were strange and improvised. Held in cramped apartments with cocky men in ripped jeans who called themselves artists, or just hunters.
Mila and her friends flirted like it was a second language. I watched them, curious, like you watch a wild animal up close. I flirted too, sometimes, but the moment anyone looked at me with hunger instead of interest, I disappeared into the wallpaper.

Mila was living with her boss. Her family, like mine, had shipped in generational fear from Algeria and told her to wear it like perfume.
Instead, she chose rebellion and picked chaos over control. It made sense to me.

When Helle visited from Copenhagen, things escalated. We saw a beach plane ad for The Gotha —Tyga was playing that night. We looked at each other and knew we were going. I invited Mila, and we all squeezed into my tiny apartment to get ready.
I kept translating between them. Kept pretending the tension I felt was just in my head.

The club was packed. My heels were killing me before we even got inside. Everyone who sat had paid for a

table. The show was loud, glittering, thick with sweat, perfume and power.
There was a kind of electricity in the air that felt ancient, almost animal. Like we were chasing something or being chased. I told myself we were just having fun. But even then, I could feel the thread starting to fray.

After a few drinks, we left around 3 or 4 a.m. too drunk to feel the warning signs.

That's when Mila got invited to an afterparty, by a guy in designer glasses and a gold chain. Mehdi. He had the kind of arrogance money buys. We said yes. The villa was massive.
A pool, a wide gate, at least two floors. It felt surreal, like walking onto Scarface's movie set.
We sat by the pool, drinking more, the conversation shallow and forgettable.
I remember thinking: *Is this it? Is this what connection looks like now?* I tried to join in when they spoke about family or work, but the rest — the men, the stuff, the endless comparisons — left me blank.
And then Mehdi disappeared. Came back. Restless. With a roll of 100-euro bills in his hand. He handed one to Mila. One to me. Then pulled out a bag. White powder. Mila didn't flinch. She carved a line on the glass table with a credit card and snorted it without ceremony.
Then she handed me the card; smoothly, casually, as if offering a piece of gum or a tampon. Something passed between us in that moment, something silent but undeniable. It wasn't peer pressure exactly; it was something more delicate, more sinister.
A kind of invitation wrapped in glitter and loneliness. I didn't want to be the girl who said no and ruined the mood, didn't want to be the one whispered about later — the boring one, the outsider, the girl who still played by

rules no one remembered writing.

And maybe, deep down, I just wanted to stop feeling like a guest in my own body.
So, I nodded. Smiled, maybe. Took the card with fingers that didn't feel like mine and leaned in like I knew what I was doing.

The line was sharp, bitter, acrid. It smelled like regret and household cleaner. Like someone had Febreezed over a grave. It sliced through my nose and settled in my throat like a lie I wasn't ready to swallow. For a moment, nothing happened — and then everything did.
The room tilted slightly, then steadied, but my body didn't catch up. My heart began thudding against my ribcage like it was trying to escape. I couldn't tell if I was floating or falling. I only knew that something in me had gone quiet: the small voice that used to say *this isn't safe*, the one I'd trained for years to ignore. This wasn't about wanting to feel good. This wasn't curiosity or rebellion.
It was about feeling *something* — anything — other than the hollow ache of disconnection.

The cocaine didn't seduce me with pleasure. It seduced me with the illusion of control, the promise that I could hold it together a little longer if I just kept moving. And in that moment, surrounded by strangers in designer lies, it felt safer to surrender than to admit how desperately alone I really was.
I told Mila I was tired, though the word didn't come close to what I felt. I was unravelling — quietly, quickly, like a thread being pulled from the inside.
I climbed the stairs one slow step at a time, each breath tighter than the last, as if the air had thickened and conspired against me. Helle was already draped in sleep and smeared mascara, like a painting left out in the rain.

I collapsed beside her, my body heavy, trembling, foreign.
The room spun in a lazy circle around me and the ceiling looked impossibly far away.

"I can't breathe," I gasped, clutching at the air like it might tear open. "Call an ambulance. Please. I think I'm dying."

"What's the number here? What is going on?" she asked, already half out of the bed, panic dragging her fully awake.

"Eighteen," I whispered. "Call eighteen."

She bolted downstairs. A moment later, Mehdi stormed back up behind her, his bravado suddenly cracked at the edges.
One glance at me, and the cool fell away.

"Don't call them," he snapped. "Fucking don't! She just needs rest!"

But I didn't need rest. I needed my lungs back. I needed the oxygen I'd traded for a sense of belonging I never actually had. I needed someone — anyone — to care more about my life than their reputation.
The ambulance came fast, though time had started playing tricks on me, stretching out in some places, folding in on itself in others. They carried me out on a stretcher, my limbs limp but my mind still twitching with fragmented thoughts. As we passed the pool, it was suddenly crowded with faces I hadn't seen all night, shadows in sequins, people who hadn't existed until emergency lights made them visible. I remember thinking, absurdly: *Where were they when I couldn't breathe?*

It was hard to tell if they came for the music or stayed for the breakdown — dignity on a stretcher, a girl-shaped cautionary tale in real time.
It was surreal.

The hospital was everything the party wasn't: cold, quiet, sterile, filled with people who didn't care who you were as long as you weren't dying on their watch. I drifted in and out until a sharp sting pulled me back — a slap across the face. Not gentle. Not kind. Just clinical, as if I were a stubborn machine refusing to reboot.
"WAKE UP," the doctor barked, and I jolted like I'd been unplugged from something sacred.
And there she was. Maya. In a nurse's gown. Watching. Saying nothing. Her eyes wide with recognition, disbelief, something like pity, but no words.

We hadn't spoken since kindergarten. She once shared her crayons with me, now she was watching a different kind of mess, older, harder to clean up. I opened my mouth to say something, anything, but the shame had lodged itself like a stone in my throat. So, we just stood there, two girls who used to draw butterflies together, now separated by years, silence, and the sour smell of shame and regret.
I wasn't just embarrassed. I was gutted. And not by the overdose, but by the fact that no one, not even God, had stepped in before I crossed the line when it was near.

Before I could be discharged, the gendarmerie showed up — two officers in plain clothes who looked more like weary teachers than enforcers of the law, but something about their presence chilled the air.
They asked me to come to the station the next day, and I nodded as if I had any real choice in the matter.

The next morning, I sat in a grey room that smelled faintly of burnt coffee and old paper. The officers were calm, almost gentle, the kind of calm that makes you feel even more exposed — like they didn't need to raise their voices to get under your skin.
They asked me where I got the cocaine.
How much I took. Who was there.
I answered everything. My hands wouldn't stop moving, folding, unfolding, gripping the edge of my jacket. My voice tripped over itself, trying to sound casual but landing somewhere between panic and apology. I didn't know how to lie. I just told them the truth, piece by shaky piece, hoping it would be enough. Or maybe hoping it wouldn't be used against me.

That's when they told me Mehdi was part of a trafficking ring based in Paris. That I had just stumbled into the middle of an active investigation.
That my overdose may have helped crack something open. I left the station in a daze, the kind that makes everything feel slightly off-kilter, like the ground is still there, but you're not sure it'll hold your weight anymore.
I called Kim in Copenhagen, and for a long time, we didn't talk about the party or the cocaine or the hospital. We talked about faith. About God. About how hard it is to keep your roots in anything solid when the ground keeps dissolving under you, like sugar in water.

A few days later, Mila called. Her voice was already sharp when I picked up.

"What the fuck did you tell the police?"

"Everything," I said. "Why? What did you say?" I didn't try to soften it. I didn't sugarcoat it. Didn't even sprinkle sarcasm on top.

"Nothing! None of us said anything. What the fuck, Luna?!" And that was it. That was the conversation. That was the end.

I hadn't realized how heavy her friendship had felt until it was gone. Funny thing... when she hung up, it wasn't grief that hit me. It was relief, and that scared me more than any threat ever could. Like I'd just slipped out of a jacket that never really fit me, but I kept wearing because it belonged to someone I could never be.

I called Kim again the next night, my voice still shaking, telling him everything. About the police. About the party. About how the Mila, and consequently, the men involved already knew where I lived — Mila had been there before.
His tone changed instantly.
"Pack your things," he said. "Now. Don't even sleep there again."
I told him I will. Left half my makeup behind. Even a pair of Gucci sunglasses I couldn't afford to lose.
"Good," he said. The next day, Mila called me, asking where I was.
"Penthouse party. Free drinks. Soooo lit. Wanna come?"
Asking to meet? After the way we left each other last time?
It wasn't a check-in.
It was a scan.

That's when I knew this wasn't paranoia.

This was how girls disappeared.

I read it to Kim, "Don't go," he said immediately, his voice low and firm. "It sounds like a setup."

So, I did the only thing that felt safe. I booked a flight back to Copenhagen, with no plan, no home. Just instinct and fear. Just the sense that if I didn't leave now, they'd find another way to make me regret telling the truth.

Kim called Jaco from Horizon Church — my old team leader. We used to serve together on Sundays, sharing coffee setups and whispered prayers before services began. Back then, he was the kind of person who made faith feel like something you could hold in your hands. When Kim explained the situation, Jaco didn't hesitate. There was a room available. A way out. A quiet place to land. I packed light, no heels, no glitter, no pretence.
Just what I could carry, and whatever was left of the girl who still believed that starting over was possible.
I zipped my suitcase like I was sealing something shut. Not a body, not exactly. But maybe a warning, or a prayer.
A promise to leave behind the part of me that kept mistaking danger for excitement, pain for love, silence for safety. I hadn't packed all that away, not really.
But I wanted to.
And sometimes, wanting is the first door you walk through.
I didn't look back when the plane lifted off.

I ran like salvation was waiting at the gate.
But not all miracles let you pass.

PART 10

ASHES & ANGELS

Chapter I

The airport was loud, but it didn't sound like anything. Not to me. The announcements echoed through the terminal like background static in a dream, and the shuffle of people — their bags, their bodies, their conversations — felt like a performance I'd been dropped into halfway through, without a script.

As I moved through security, my lips started trembling, not from the cold. My eyes teared up just from looking at someone, anyone. A glance from a stranger could unravel me. I passed by the duty-free liquor shelves like a ghost, my body dragging behind me. I wanted to drink. Not to feel better, but to *feel something.* Or maybe nothing. Anything other than the ache pooling in my chest. But I didn't. It wasn't self-restraint or some hard-won lesson. I was just exhausted — tired of the loop where pain gets postponed, only to return louder, drunker, and heavier the next morning. The truth is, I'd already begun rehearsing what vanishing might feel like. I didn't want the wine. I wanted the silence it could never deliver.

People in the airport moved with purpose —businessmen, backpackers, families whose passports looked nothing alike — all walking like they knew exactly where they were going. I envied that: a destination, a plan, a reason to keep moving forward when everything in me wanted to stop. It made me ache in the way only beauty does. The fact that all these lives, from all these places, were stitched together here in a moment that would dissolve as quickly as it formed... there was something holy about it. Something unbearably tender.

At the gate, I saw a mother with her toddler, he was mid-meltdown, cheeks flushed, fists curled. She pulled him close, and his tiny body collapsed into hers like it remembered something ancient: safety. He cried for five minutes, then slept like he'd never known pain.

I couldn't look away or envy her. I just saw something too tender to hold.

In that moment, I understood with clarity that I would never be a mother. Not because I couldn't, but because I couldn't imagine inflicting *me* on a child. I didn't want to hand someone a map with no safe place marked.

I was still trying to survive myself. I was the trap. And it would be cruel to invite a child into that. I thought, not with malice, but with a deep, exhausted conviction: this suffering should have ended before it began. Maybe my mother should have ended it when she had the chance. Maybe the act of creation was the original betrayal.

I felt hungry as I waited, but it wasn't food I was after. It was the kind of hunger that sharpened you. It was power disguised as punishment. A voice inside whispered, *you're alone, you're broken, you will always be alone,* and starving felt like proof. Like I could control at least this much.

I stared out the window at the clouds — endless and weightless, like a place made only for the forgiven. They looked like land from above, but gentler. Somewhere

you could rest without having to explain why you were tired.
Maybe the clouds are just beds for the people who wanted to live. And I'm here, wide awake, carrying a tiredness even death would understand.
I smiled, not out of peace, but because it confirmed something I'd always suspected: maybe some of us were never meant to rest. I'd always had this feeling I wouldn't make it past twenty-five. That wasn't a fear. It was a comfort. A deadline. Something to count on.
As I looked out at the endless white sky, it felt confirmed — the way a prophecy does. I'd carried the wish to end everything since I was a child, but it had never felt so near, so reachable, so... gentle.
No one knew. And somehow, that made death feel less like an escape and more like a secret destination I'd always been heading toward — quietly, deliberately and without a map.

When I arrived in Copenhagen, Jaco met me at the door of the house Kim had helped me find.
He was warm. Gentle in that unassuming, church-team-leader way. We hugged. He seemed genuinely happy that someone would finally be filling the last room in the house. I smiled.
The house was a bit old, with a staircase leading to the front door. Inside, it opened into a modest hallway, and past the living room was a sunroom that spilled out onto a wide terrace. It wasn't perfect, but it didn't need to be. My room had a bed, a cupboard, and a table with a chair. That was enough. That was always enough. I'd never learned to want more than that.
I didn't decorate the walls. I never had. Not because I saw it as a chore, but because I genuinely didn't know how.

The idea of frames, colours, "accent pieces", those were things for people who had been told their existence deserved beauty. I didn't know how to make a room mine. I barely knew how to make a life mine.

Andrew lived across the hall. Loud, magnetic, full of life. The kind of laugh that made you look up even if you were mid-cry. We became fast friends. We often joked about the other roommate — a girl who lived in the room beside mine, who hadn't shown her face once in the entire month I'd been there. One night, we heard a thud from her room. I turned to Andrew and asked if that could be our mysterious roommate. Without missing a beat, and with a completely straight face, he said, "It would be more probable to be a rat." I laughed harder than I had in weeks. I couldn't wait to meet her. It would be nice to have another woman around. Balance the energy. Maybe talk about something other than protein powder.

But balance wasn't coming.

–

One night, Helle and I got invited to a houseboat party. Joe, a mutual friend from church, texted us. Joe was warm, animated, one of those people who made you feel like you'd known them for years after five minutes. He didn't know what had happened in France. He just knew I was back.
The boat was docked at the harbor, lit up like a movie set. Inside, it smelled of cocktails and cigarettes, but the interior was sleek and expensive. Copenhagen does this thing in autumn where it pretends its winter — biting cold air, pitch-black evenings at 5 p.m. But inside the boat, it was warm. Intoxicating in every sense. The guests were few but unforgettable.

A quiet man with the air of a veteran; blonde, mid-thirties, haunted around the eyes, and a woman with surgically sculpted cheekbones and sadness hiding beneath the lip filler. The owner of the boat wore a white shirt and carried himself like he owned more than just the water.
They were kind. Disarmed in that specific way people get after 10 p.m., just enough alcohol to let their pain speak, but not enough to admit they're listening to it.

The cocaine showed up an hour in. The veteran had disappeared into a back room and came out with a plate. Neat white lines. As he re-entered, something shifted in the atmosphere. Time didn't stop, but it *paused,* like it was asking permission. Everyone took a line. Everyone but Helle and Joe. I later found out Joe was a recovering addict who'd become allergic to cocaine. At the time, I didn't ask. I just watched.
My eyes fixated on the plate. I told myself I wouldn't. Not tonight. Not in front of Helle. I didn't want her to witness me ruin something again.

But the night stretched. The veteran kept disappearing. And finally, I followed.

We took a line together in the back. The second it hit, I felt it — clean, cold, merciful. My heart pounded, but not in fear. My breath moved in and out like I was finally part of something in rhythm. I felt still. Calm. Like the static had been shut off.

I turned to him and asked, "How do I get more?"
He gave me a number.

From that moment on, I didn't live. I floated.

There's a moment when drugs stop being a detour and become your address. Mine came with silk curtains and a view of nothing I wanted to see.
My sole mission was to reduce the volume of my existence, until I was ready to put an end to it. I didn't want to *solve* my problems. I just wanted to dull the constant sound they made.

People think addicts are chasing highs. They're not. We're chasing *relief.* Because here's what no one tells you: addiction rarely starts as pleasure. It starts as survival.
When the sound of a door handle swinging makes your entire nervous system brace for impact, when the soft swish of a shower curtain means you've got thirty seconds before your mother steps out and ruins the rest of the day, even when you mother is thousands of kilometres away — you're not getting high to escape. You're getting high to stay alive without falling apart.
I didn't want bliss. I wanted silence. And now.

Joe delivered the first bag. Said he knew a guy. I told myself it was a one-time thing. It wasn't.
I kept the bag tucked into my pillowcase, like a bitter little secret I was cradling to sleep. I started using once a day, then twice. Sometimes less, if I was rationing. October blurred. A beautiful kind of blur. The kind you fall in love with because it doesn't ask questions.
Sometimes, a breeze would slip through the window, carrying the bite of cold air mixed with the faint trace of cigarettes — and suddenly, I was back on the boat. Not really, but enough for my body to forget. I'd hear a laugh through the wall or the clink of glass from the kitchen, and my brain would stitch the sounds into that night: the warm lights, the sharp powder, the quiet ache behind every smile.

It scared me, how easily my senses could trick me. How one night I barely meant to live through had become the one my body wanted to return to. Again, that's the thing about addiction — it doesn't need repetition. Just a single moment of relief is enough for the mind to mark it as home. Even if it kills you.

The more I used, the less I wanted to stop. Not because it felt good, but because sobriety started to feel like drowning. I didn't want to be alert. I wanted someone — anyone — to take my head in their hands, look me in the eye, and ask something soft. Something only a mother would know to say.

Maybe: *"Baby, when did it start to hurt so much?"*

I wanted to be held, tight, for days. Long enough for my heartbeat to forget its panic. Long enough for me to believe that love didn't come with a price tag or a bruise.

I kept seeing Sarah and Kim. Kept going to church. Sometimes I'd see the football player and rush to the bathroom. I'd do a line. Return. Smile. Hug people. Praise God. I didn't feel guilt anymore. I was past that. I was an extrovert in the lobby and a ghost in the stall.

I asked people how they were. Really asked. Listened like it mattered. Because I needed someone to do the same. And when they didn't, giving that care to others almost felt like enough. But I stopped going eventually. When you're too numb to feel shame, there's no point in pretending you belong in a place built on redemption.

That autumn, I watched the people at the boat party laugh more as they drank more. They joked about their traumas like they were sitcom episodes —vulnerability diluted with punchlines, heavy truths cut off just before the silence settled. But I saw it in their eyes. The way their gaze dropped for half a second after a sentence.

The way they stared at nothing before jolting back into the party like actors missing their cues.
I didn't envy them.
I recognized them.
We were the same. Not alone in our loneliness, which made it almost worse. Like our sadness had formed a club no one applied to, but everyone joined anyway.

And I was finally a member.

I still showed up to social gatherings and events, but I could feel myself slipping further from the version of me that existed before the plate, before the veteran, before I mistook stillness for healing. I never used at parties. Not around people. Only when I was alone — in my room, behind a closed door, the bag tucked into my pillowcase like something sacred and shameful. It made me feel safer that way, more in control somehow, like I could still draw a line between coping and collapsing.
Addiction is clever. Like a bad boyfriend with a PhD in gaslighting; by the time you realize you're isolated, it's already convinced you it was your idea.
The silence deepened, but I kept calling it peace. I told myself it was better this way, it was less mess, less worry, less chance of disappointing anyone who still cared. Sometimes I thought about saying something. About opening my mouth and letting the truth fall out. But then I'd imagine their faces with all the concern, the advice, the inevitable question of why I hadn't told them sooner, and I'd go quiet again. Not because I didn't want to be helped, but because I couldn't explain why I needed the numbness more than I needed saving.

Chapter 2

We met properly in the living room. I was sitting with my guitar, half-playing, half-hiding behind the chords. She stepped out of her room and into the sunlight like it had been waiting for her. She lifted a hand to greet me, and I stood up and hugged her instead. She blinked — surprised, maybe amused — like she hadn't expected to be met with arms instead of words. Maybe it was my extroversion. Or maybe just the relief of finally giving the mystery girl behind the door a face.

Tall. Striking. Canadian. She wore those facts like loose jewelry — they caught the light, but didn't define her. Her family had lived in this house when they moved back from Canada, and the way she said it, made it feel like history still hung in the air. She asked about the guitar, and I sang. Not to impress — okay, definitely to impress — but because she asked like someone who genuinely *wanted* to hear. Not even to fill the silence or to be polite. The kind of asking that feels like an invitation, not an obligation.

When she moved toward the piano, it was like watching someone return home. Her fingers touched the keys like they remembered something her mouth couldn't say, and her voice wrapped around the room like a blanket. I wanted her fingers to stay on the keys forever, and her voice to echo in places I didn't know needed warmth.

We didn't talk every day. Not deliberately. Just enough for gravity to start forming between us. She didn't waste time with small talk. Her questions carried weight — not invasive, just intentional.

The way she cared didn't ask for anything in return. And I didn't know what to do with that. With someone who noticed what even *I* was trying not to see.

I don't remember the specifics of our early conversations. Just the warmth — the blur of being seen without needing to perform. That's how memory works during addiction; even the important moments fold into each other like a bad dreams. But I remember how I felt when she looked at me. Not as if I were broken, but as if she had already decided I was worth staying curious about.

Then, one evening — the staircase.

I was smoking when she sat down beside me. But she joined me on my left. Close. No space for pretending. She didn't ask for permission, she just arrived and looked at me like she was reading a language I'd forgotten I was speaking. Her eyes didn't drift. Her posture didn't shift. She just stayed, with a stillness that made my skin itch and my guard drop. And then she asked something — something simple, maybe about my day, or my family, or if I was okay — but she asked it like the answer mattered more than the question.
I told her everything. About the drugs. The lines. The pillow. I hadn't meant to. My mouth took over before my mind could object. It came out fast, but not messy. It came out like truth that had been waiting for a soft enough place to land.

She didn't flinch. Didn't interrupt. Didn't rush to meet my story with her own. She just listened like it was her job to hold the silence open. Her arms wrapped around me, her presence steady, her eyes doing the quiet work of twenty therapists — not the kind who write notes and nod, but the kind who knows silence is sometimes the only thing loud enough to be heard.

I had told Jaco too, soon after I moved in — because he needed to know what he was signing up for. He'd nodded, offered support, told me to reach out if I needed. And that mattered. But this... this was different. Bella didn't offer support. She offered presence. And that felt rarer than love.

When I went back to my room, I panicked. I regretted telling her. Not because she didn't respond with grace, but because I couldn't believe someone would see all that and still stay. I sat at the edge of my bed, my knees pulled in, the pillow holding its secret stash behind my back. My body was heavy, but not from shame. From the sheer weight of having been heard. That in itself was exhausting — like being held up just long enough to realize how long you've been collapsing. When you carry pain alone for years, being seen isn't always a relief. It's disarming. It peels back the armor you forgot you were wearing, and suddenly everything hurts more. Not because you're weaker, but because you're finally safe enough to feel it. Because when you're used to people needing something from you, kindness feels like a trick. You keep waiting for the bill. The terms. A shift. But the bill didn't come. Just her, still there — ruining every rule I'd written about what love was supposed to cost.
Bella didn't shift.
She didn't change after that.
She didn't treat me like a cause.
Didn't treat my honesty like a job application for her empathy.
She just let it be there, between us.
She didn't text inspirational quotes.
She didn't tiptoe.
She didn't distance herself either.
She just... stayed the same.
Maybe a little more attentive, a little gentler.

But it was like she'd known who I was all along and had just been waiting for me to catch up.
She started checking in, quietly. And I started walking slower.

Just enough to notice the light.

But somewhere in the silence, the end had already begun. I just hadn't noticed the knock yet.

Chapter 3

It was a Sunday. The kind that watches you from the corner. Everyone had gone to church. I stayed. Not out of defiancc or rest, but because I could. That kind of freedom, when you're already slipping, doesn't feel like liberty, but more like an unlocked door on a windy night.
Bella, Jaco and Andrew left for church with their usual warmth and shoes still slightly wet from morning dew. Their absence wasn't loud. It was habitual. And that was the hardest part. I stayed behind, blanketed in silence that didn't feel like solitude, it felt like I'd been left behind by a world still spinning. I turned on music, hoping sound might drown the echo that had started taking root in my chest. But the volume didn't matter. The loneliness was louder. My favorite series played in the background, the kind I usually used like a blanket.

But that day, it played to no one. My eyes were open, but nothing landed. Instead, there was a sound. Low, rhythmic, sharp around the edges.
Huh. Huh. Huh.

The sound of my mother slapping her own cheeks during her psychotic meltdowns — that breathless wheeze, sharp and desperate, that always split the air a few seconds before she lost control. I hadn't become her, not exactly. But the flashbacks were back. And I couldn't outrun what had already made a home in me. I hadn't thought about that particular sound in years, but suddenly it was in the room with me, as if she'd left it there like a curse. It looped through my mind, synchronized with the pressure building behind my ribs, and I wasn't mocking her. I was mirroring her. Helplessness passed down like a family heirloom no one wanted to claim. That same internal scream was looking for an exit, but I didn't slap myself. I reached for the three grams of cocaine tucked under my pillow like a secret scripture, reverent in the ritual. It felt holy, almost like an act of communion with the only god that hadn't left.

I didn't hesitate. It felt like being reunited with my one reliable god — one that didn't ask questions, didn't require explanations.

My fingers moved faster than my thoughts. I carved out a thick line. My jaw trembled. My mouth moved without meaning to. Tears gathered, not out of sadness, but the strange relief that comes when your body finally feels heard, from the kind of grief that floods quietly.

I told myself it would be just one line. Just enough to dull the sharp edge. But when it hit, and I sank into the stillness and peace it gave me — that familiar, anaesthetic quiet — something in me wanted more. Wanted deeper. I wanted all of it. Another line, then another. My hands shook, clumsy with hunger. I wasn't even inside myself anymore. Just hovering, watching the shell move. My body had already decided.

My mind just followed, slow and stunned, like a child being dragged through a panic. The pain had outgrown language. Sorrow had shed its language.

All that was left was chemistry and compulsion.

And that sound.

Huh. Huh. Huh.

The blood coursed so fast I felt it in my scalp, hot and electric, like my hair was being pulled from the inside out. I hated it. I needed it gone. So, I told myself one more — one final line to cancel out the last three. I emptied the last of the bag, leveled it with my bank card, and inhaled like I was trying to vanish from the inside out.

And then my throat began to close.

It wasn't a pain. It wasn't a jolt. It was something more terrifying — the absence of sensation. Like anaesthesia bleeding into every cell. I couldn't breathe, and yet there was no gasping. No struggle. Only a narrowing, like a hallway closing in. My heart wasn't racing. It was hammering at something far deeper. My chest pulsed with such force I thought maybe it wasn't my heart at all, maybe it was the entire memory of me trying to push its way out.

I was soaked, shaking, crawling across the room as my muscles locked and twisted.

Here!

My phone, I found it.

My hands wouldn't cooperate, but somehow, I got the number out.

"Now," I told myself. *"You can go now. It's quiet enough."*

It wasn't a plea. It was a decision. This time, death didn't knock; it entered softly, almost politely, like it had been waiting for me to make up my mind.

The hours between that moment and the 911 call

stretched in strange directions; bent time, swollen with memory and blackout. But even as death hovered, life tried to continue. Again, that's the awful thing about addiction. You can be dying in your own body and still make polite conversation on Tuesday.

Joe kept coming through — same day, same smile.
No questions. We both pretended this wasn't lethal. That this wasn't some sort of a murder ritual in slow motion. He handed me poison like it was perfume. I paid like I was buying gum. Just product and politeness. Maybe he didn't want to know. Maybe he preferred the version of me who texted emojis and thanked him like we were sharing something harmless. I was buying enough to tranquilize a stable, and he still thought I was "a weekend user."
It was easier than explaining how survival sometimes looks like destruction, just with better manners.
If Sarah had known how bad it really was, and especially that it was her good friend Joe supplying me, she would've panicked. So, I kept her at arm's length, but not in distance — in information. It was easier than explaining how survival sometimes looks like destruction, just with better manners.
We were still close, still joking. Sarah and I were chaos in harmony, kind of like mismatched socks that somehow made the outfit work. We could find humour in almost anything, usually things we absolutely shouldn't. She'd start a sentence and forget halfway through what she was saying, and I'd interrupt with something equally nonsensical, and we'd both laugh like it was the smartest thing we'd heard all week. We weren't always making sense, but we made space. And that was enough. There was something childlike about us — like two kids building a fort out of sarcasm and side-eyes. No one else was allowed in, and even we didn't always know what we were defending ourselves from.

Eventually, I told Sarah. Then Kim. And as I anticipated, they carried the kind of worry that adds years to their face. Not wrinkles, but weight. But they didn't really understand why I kept using.
I tried to explain once, that addiction wasn't about pleasure, or rebellion, or chaos. It was about mercy.
It was the only thing that made the pain bearable without asking me to name it. That's the cruelty of it — you're not running toward euphoria. You're running from memory, from noise, from your own goddamn skin. And every time you use, you're punished for surviving. But they didn't understand, they didn't know what the drug gave me. If they knew about the silence it offered, the suspension of gravity, then maybe they'd understand I wasn't addicted to cocaine. I was addicted to the absence of pain.

Bella, though, she had a different access point. She never asked me to stop. She didn't perform concern like a moral checklist. She never cornered me with confrontation because I was already living in a corner. She saw through it. Through me. Not in the way people claim to, not the romantic kind of "seeing" someone. No, she saw the wreckage, the rot, the way I had become fluent in silence and disguised in obedience. And she stayed anyway.
We had grown close by then, slowly, cautiously. I still had walls, but she had a way of reading me that didn't require blueprints. She never forced her way in. She just lingered long enough that I started to forget why I'd built the wall in the first place.
She never confronted me about my use. I think she understood that I already knew it was destroying me. She didn't try to fix me. She loved me instead. Fully. Without condition. She saw that what I lacked wasn't discipline — it was a reason to believe I deserved gentleness. And she gave it, anyway. She was already

showing up for someone I couldn't bear to be.
One night, we were lying in her bed. She told me about her own anxiety, about the things in her life that were pulling her thin. Her words were soft but solid — like she was building a bridge just by being honest. She tensed after she spoke, as if worried it had been too much. I didn't say anything.
I just moved toward her, draped my body over hers, wrapped my arms around her. We didn't speak for a long time. The silence wasn't awkward. It was sacred. But it was hard to let in love like that. Because it clashed with the part of me that still planned to leave. Sometimes I'd catch a glimpse of something warm in the darkness — a future, a choice, a reason — and then I'd shut it down before it could expand. Hope didn't fit in the architecture of my grief.
And in that quiet, I felt her breathing slow. Mine did too. Our nervous systems untangled, just a little. Something softened. It made everything more unbearable — not because of pain, but because of hope. That night, something in me flinched. I didn't want softness. I couldn't afford it. I had already made a deal with death, and her presence complicated it. It's hard to plan your escape while someone is gently placing their hand over the latch. I started to see glimpses of light. That was the problem. I didn't want to see the world get warm again, I wouldn't survive the disappointment if it went cold.
I don't know what exactly began that night. But I knew I wasn't ready for what would become.
I asked her sometimes, with more bitterness than I meant to: "Why are you still here?" I'd list all the things I wasn't; stable, sober, grateful. I wasn't a friend; I was a liability. And she'd just stare at me. Five seconds, maybe ten. That look — heavy with kindness and certainty and exhaustion. "You've given me more than you realize," she'd say. "This is not a one-way friendship." She never told me exactly what she meant. But I know what it's like

to feel useful in someone else's pain. To make yourself essential so you don't feel disposable. Maybe we both needed to be needed. Maybe that's why we held on.
But watching me self-destruct wasn't passive. It broke something in her too. I could see it. And I still let it happen. I couldn't stop.
But life doesn't wait for readiness, grief or healing.
The overdoses kept coming, soft and slow like tides. Each time I thought this would be it. This one will work. This time I'll go where the quiet is permanent. But no. My body, fragile and thin as it was, kept clawing back to the surface.

And one Sunday, I didn't scream. I just stopped holding myself together. The overdoses didn't stop. I had many — too many. One of them was just as deadly. And after each one, it was Bella who came. The hospitals had her number now. She became my next of kin, not because I asked her to be, but because she decided I was hers.

That night, when all of them went to church, I had written a note. Triple the dose. No fanfare. No tragedy. I dialed 911, like a reflex I didn't mean to honor. And then I changed my mind. I decided to lay down and let it end. Between the call and the answer, something in me gave up, not with ceremony or clarity, but with the slow unraveling that happens when despair and apathy blur into one. That's the thing people rarely understand about suicide: it's not a clean, forward-moving decision, but a collapsing hallway of contradiction, where the urge to be saved exists right alongside the longing to disappear. I didn't want to be rescued. I didn't want to be dead. I just couldn't bear another moment of being awake inside that pain.
I remember barely breathing, my body already pulling away from itself, and still, a thought surfaced — slow and strangely practical: if I was going to be found, better it be

by strangers in uniforms than by Bella, or Jaco, or Andrew. I didn't want their hands on my body like that. I didn't want them to carry the image of me as a headline. If someone was going to see me like that — limp, used up, already halfway gone — let it be someone who wouldn't have to remember the same way they would.

But then — a voice, sudden and clear, slicing through the fog: "911, this is the central alarm. What is your emergency?"

I don't remember what I said, just that it was good enough. Maybe my address. Maybe my name.

"Can you open the door for the paramedics? Stay with me. They're coming."

Her voice was steady. She repeated herself often, gently, like a rope tossed into water. I held on. Crawled toward the front door, my phone still clutched. Even then, I worried about making noise. Lenny was living illegally in the basement, and if they found out, it could ruin everything for him.

Even while dying, I worried about being a burden.

I got to the door. I don't remember opening it.

The next thing I remember is the ceiling; the old, white one with tiny flecks, not textured or smooth, it was just... there. My eyes locked on it, and my vision was like a dying television screen. I still see that ceiling sometimes, in random moments. Not as a memory, but a mirror. A reminder that some part of me stayed there, blinking through static, waiting for the signal to return. Fuzzy static creeping in from the corners. That grainy black-and-white snow you see when a channel goes dead.

"Luna? Are you here?" There were knocks. Then footsteps coming up the basement stairs. I hadn't opened the door after all, instead, they found me collapsed against it, trying to open.

Lenny must have let them in.

"We have her," someone said.

And after that — flashes.
Being lifted. A man's arms under me. A rush of cold air against my skin. The blinding ambulance lights. Five people talking, moving, touching, attaching things to me, around me, through me. I could see them. Hear them. But I couldn't make my body react.
And then, they all stopped.
The silence was instant, heavy. I wasn't breathing. I wasn't screaming. Just... present. Watching.
My thoughts screamed silently:
Please don't stop. I'm still in here. I'm not gone. I'm not gone.
But no one moved. I thought — this is it. I'll be conscious forever, but unreachable. Buried in a body that can't scream. I thought I was dead.
Then the sirens started.
The ambulance moved.
And I thought — through the roar of the world trying to resuscitate me:
This is what resurrection sounds like. And it's louder than hell.
I knew I couldn't keep going. But I didn't know how to stop. And that's the thing about despair... it doesn't kill you cleanly. It waits for you to hope, and then it reminds you why you shouldn't have.
I slipped into something that felt eerily close to sleep. No darkness, or pain. Just a quiet blankness, like the screen turning off mid-scene. I don't remember anything after that.
When I woke up — again — I didn't feel relief. I felt rage. I felt shame.
I had rehearsed the ending, recited it like scripture, and still, I survived.
I wanted to scream. But all I could do was cry.
Bella found the note. I don't remember what she said. But I remember what her face looked like. She didn't cry in front of me. But I think she had already started grieving me in advance. She never said she was done. But I could feel her heart bracing for the final call.

And still... Bella stayed.
They said I was lucky, but I wasn't sure luck was the word. Survival, when it isn't your choice, feels less like grace and more like debris; the kind of rubble you crawl out from with limbs that no longer work and a heart that keeps going only out of habit.

During the lockdown, the world went silent. And for the first time, I couldn't distract myself. No job. No appointments. No crowd to disappear into. I was left alone with myself, and I had no idea how to survive that. I had money left from Cannes. The fridge was full. The world was closed, and so was I.
The fog in my brain thickened. My body withered. I don't remember most of that year. What I do recall is that Bella didn't leave. We lived in emotional whiplash; woke up in grief, went to bed in laughter. We ate meals like confessions and watched Netflix like it might save us. It felt like sisterhood. It *was* sisterhood.
And yet, I still tried to die the day before my birthday.
It didn't work. Again. (I was starting to feel like the world's most inconsistent magician: now you see me, now... nope. Still here.)
At this point, even death seemed annoyed. Like, "Girl, get it together... I've got a schedule."
I laughed at the thought, and then it hit me: I didn't want to make it to twenty-one. It didn't mark anything sacred, it just felt like crossing a finish line into more of the same. More mornings to negotiate with. More furniture that judged me. More people saying they loved me as long as I kept performing a version of myself that they could understand.
Bella had planned everything: a cake, decorations, and invitations to friends she'd quietly coordinated like it was a covert op. She told everyone not to mention anything about the incident directly to me. If they had something to say, they had to go through her.

Not because she was trying to micromanage joy, but because she knew what a minefield it was. She knew I could detonate at the sound of well-meaning affection. She wasn't planning a party. She was staging a rescue mission disguised as celebration, layering safety into lasagna and candlelight, hoping I'd believe I deserved to stay. She wanted the day to feel like something I didn't have to earn. Like maybe I could belong to it, maybe I could stay.

At some point during the party, I remember saying out loud, "I feel stupid. How can I want to die, everything is not so bad." And everyone nodded with that kind of smile people give when they don't know how to respond without making it worse. But that was the thing, it wasn't bad. It just wasn't bearable. There's a difference. And it's the kind that makes you feel like the problem isn't your life, it's *you*.

I felt so guilty that I didn't want to be awake on the day she tried so hard to give me. I wanted to sleep through it. Or disappear into it.

Because the thing about pain is: it doesn't care if you're loved. It doesn't care how many people gather around your table, or how hard someone fought to cook your favourite lasagna. It just wants to leave. And when it can't, it tries to take you with it. Love never stood a chance against that kind of precision. Pain has better aim. It doesn't wait for birthday candles or surprise parties. It just sharpens itself until even kindness feels like a threat. Until you start apologizing for being celebrated. Until the thought of another year feels more like a dare than a gift. And survival feels like a punishment for the people trying to make you stay.

I didn't want to unbox another morning. Hope is cruel that way, because it keeps offering tomorrows even when you've stopped asking.

Bella was devastated. And tired. I think she started preparing herself for the call. She never said it. But I

could see it in her eyes, it wasn't just sorrow, but resignation.
The worst part wasn't that I almost died. It was that I nearly did, and part of me still wanted to. That ache didn't vanish with the IV drip or the sirens. It lingered, quiet and patient, like it knew I'd be back.

And maybe I would've been, if not for the sound of her voice on the other end of the line, steady, human, unwilling to let me disappear without a witness.

Chapter 4

After the second overdose, there wasn't just one more. There were many. More than I could count. More than anyone knew. Each one blurred into the next like the aftershocks of an earthquake that never fully stops.
But by then, Bella was no longer just my roommate. She was my emergency contact.
In any other life, the hospital would've reached for a parent, or someone official, someone blood. But mine weren't in the Danish system. No CPR number. No emergency line. No one to call. So, they called Bella. And she came. Every time.
No matter the hour, or the reason. Even when the reasons stopped making sense. Even when the calls came more often than sleep. She came — sometimes with her shoes on the wrong feet, sometimes in tears, but always steady enough to hold my hand.
When the lockdown started, everything that kept me distracted evaporated. The world went quiet, but inside me, the storm only grew louder. Cafés closed. The hospitality and restaurant industry shut down. Bella

found a job at a school eventually, but I had nothing. No income. No routine. No stage to perform on. Just the silence of our shared house and the leftover savings from my time in Cannes.
I had always kept myself orbiting around chaos or numbing myself away from it, but never this. Never face-to-face with it in full daylight. I didn't know then that this is what withdrawal from distraction feels like. Not just from drugs, but from the side of myself I'd been feeding — the one that looked functional enough to get through each day.
I had made peace with dying. Not in a dramatic, cinematic way... just in the quiet, exhausted sense that I no longer belonged here. But not like this. Not while Bella was still tethered to my name, still picking up the phone every time the hospital called, still bracing herself to be the one who got the final call. That's what made it harder, it wasn't the dying but knowing someone I loved might have to witness it.
It wasn't supposed to be her grief. She had her own ghosts. But mine kept calling her phone. She was listed as my next of kin, and that's what addiction had turned her into, a part-time school worker, full-time disaster hotline for one emotionally unstable raccoon in human form.

I don't remember much from that time. Not clearly. The drugs fogged everything; my mind, my memory, my ability to string a week together. But I remember us — Bella and I — trying to make life inside that silence. Everything was closed. I was out of reasons to pretend. No more cafés, no more restaurants, no more distractions. Just the house, the fog, and Bella.
We managed to make the days tolerable. No, we made them beautiful. Despite everything. We had so much fun. We'd sit by the stairs where I first opened up to her, chain-smoking and talking.

About everything and nothing. She missed her friends in Canada, I missed my sister in France. We'd talk about what it does to the nervous system, missing someone that much. How it wears you out like grief. And then we'd ask ourselves which one of us was more likely to end up in a gang — Bella said me, obviously, because I had the trauma resume for it. I said her, because she had the face no one would suspect. It was a stupid, running joke. But it gave our grief somewhere to hide. We'd spiral from pain into play and back again.

But I remember the feeling of my bones pressing against the mattress, brushing my teeth and feeling the toothbrush scraping the inside of my cheeks because my face had sunken. I remember standing at the window and wondering how long a person could be hollow before disappearing altogether.

What I do remember — what remains unblurred — is Bella. Us, wrapped in blankets on the living room floor like kids hiding from war. Laughing so hard our faces ached. Dancing barefoot to terrible music. Laying our feet on the fridge laying on the floor, while Jaco passed and asked: What the hell? Before we burst out laughing. She brought me into her life, introduced me to her family, her friends, made me feel like I still existed outside my addiction. And in that house, during a time when the world was closed, she made a home out of ruin.

But even then, the fear never left her. Not really.

Every time I wasn't home, she lived with the quiet terror that the hospital would call again. That it would be the last time. That she'd be the one asked to identify me.

This is what addiction does, it doesn't ask you what you want, but it gives your nervous system what it expects. Pain, followed by temporary mercy. That's all it is.

A loop. Not desire, not rebellion; just a body trained to reach for its abuser because, for a moment, it stops hurting.

It doesn't just break the user, it bleeds fear into the people who love you until their sleep, their joy, even their silences reek of it.
And somehow, I knew that. I knew exactly what it was doing to her. And I still used. It was not out of spite. Not even out of need. But because the idea of stopping was so far from my reality, it felt fictional.

Addiction is not chaos. It's routine. It's ritual. It's sitting on a park bench in spring sunlight and using because you don't know what else to do with your hands. It's snorting in a church bathroom between hymns. It's scheduling your next hit in the back of a hospital hallway, right after they've wheeled you out of surgery for appendicitis.
It's promising yourself: this is the last time, while your hands are already preparing the next one.
It is a life lived in parentheses.

I believed my case was sealed. That I was one of the lost ones. Again, I didn't want to die, I just couldn't imagine a version of myself that could live anymore.
My twentieth birthday was coming up. I told myself I would wait. That I'd give myself that milestone before disappearing. But I couldn't wait. Not really.

After my attempt the day before my birthday, Bella's face was different. Not angry. Just worn. That kind of sorrow that doesn't cry anymore. Just prepares. She didn't say it. But I knew. She was trying to accept it before it happened, like softening the blow would make it easier to carry.
And I wanted to tell her she didn't have to. That she could leave, at any time. That I would understand. But I didn't want her to go either. She was the only person still standing at the edge of the cliff with me. And even though she was tired, she stayed.

She stayed.

If I could go back to those nights, the ones where we smoked on the stairs and talked about missing people who were still alive, I would've told her the truth.

That sometimes, she was the only proof I had that I wasn't already gone. A mirror held up to the ghost I'd become.
And maybe, maybe that's all it takes at first. Not hope, or healing, just the unbearable ache of being witnessed before you're ready to be found.
Some bruises don't fade; they sink deeper, until even you can't tell where the pain ends and the person begins. But sometimes, someone sees you anyway. Even when you've disappeared so completely, you start to wonder if you were ever real at all.

Chapter 5

There's something cruel about the way people start looking at you once you've fallen too far for their comfort. Like pain turns contagious, and fear — especially the well-meaning, Christian kind — puts on judgment like a mask, pretending it's protection.
When Jaco's girlfriend, Lina, moved into our shared house, she slipped into his room like she'd always belonged there. Her toothpaste sat next to his overnight, her shampoo occupied the corner of the tub, and her presence began to shape the house without trying. It was around then that the house stopped feeling like a shared space and started feeling like a stage I wasn't welcome

on.
At first, it didn't feel threatening. We'd met for coffee once back when I still went to church. I'd even taught her a few French phrases, laughing together over how to explain the absurdity of conjugation to an English tongue. I thought we were friends.
And maybe we had been, in that brief moment before fear taught her to look through me.
But addiction changes the furniture in a room. People start walking differently around you, like they don't want to wake the thing they think you've become. Lina started ignoring me entirely. No greetings. No smiles. Just silence and careful avoidance, as if I'd suddenly become a hallway, she didn't feel safe walking down.
I let it happen. I was used to being left behind.
Over time, Jaco's behaviour shifted, too. What was once mildly cold grew sharper, like he'd picked up Lina's fear.
One evening, Bella came into my room with that look — the one that warned of something unkind, even if it was said gently. Jaco had told her Lina was "afraid of drugs."
Which was fair. Who wouldn't be? But what I couldn't understand was how she treated me as if I *was* the drug. As if I were a walking bag of white powder that had learned to speak English and make coffee. I wasn't a person in pain; I was the pain itself.
Her fear was never of the overdose. It was of *me*. And I think that broke something quiet inside me. That was the cruelty of it. They didn't fear death. They feared me, like I was its messenger.
She was the kind of girl who hung Bible verses in the living room and kept a journaling Bible next to her oat milk. The type that underlined "love is patient" while actively unseeing everyone that made love inconvenient. The kind who thinks love thy neighbor comes with a footnote: unless they're foaming on your bathroom floor. One day, Bella told me that Jaco and Lina had privately said they were scared I might steal cash from

their room. That did it. That snapped something.
I would have sold my kidney before stealing a single fucking coin from anyone in that house.

The contrast between them and Bella was devastating. Bella saw *through* the curtain of addiction, she saw the me beneath it. But Jaco and Lina? They stared at the curtain like it was all there was. Like I had disappeared behind it entirely, and the only thing left was a shape they couldn't trust. It was like they'd mistaken the symptom for the soul. And somehow, that hurt more than any withdrawal ever had.
People think addiction turns you into someone else. It doesn't. It just makes it easier for them to pretend you never existed. Some would probably say their fear was understandable; that if I was desperate enough, I might steal. And sure, desperation makes people do reckless things. But addiction doesn't erase your values. It doesn't rewrite your entire moral code overnight. It just dulls your ability to care about yourself, not about right and wrong. I didn't lose my integrity when I lost control. I lost safety. I lost stability. But I never stopped knowing the difference between survival and betrayal. And I never would have crossed that line.
Not even when I wanted to disappear.

There was a time, not long after, when Matty came to visit. Matty, from The Last Reformation. One of the old soldier saints. He was kind once, but religion had carved his kindness into conviction. He sat in our living room with Kim and Sarah, sipping coffee and sermonizing in soft tones about missions, repentance, rebirth. His words weren't mean, but they carried a weight, like they believed themselves holy even while hovering in the atmosphere.
As he spoke, my body started to hum with that familiar electricity, that shame disguised as static. I don't know

what part of me snapped. Maybe it was the hypocrisy. Maybe it was the echo of my own voice from years before, preaching the same righteous extremism. And now here I was, barely upright, craving dope and trying to stay conscious long enough to fake small talk. I excused myself.

In the mirror of the bathroom, I didn't see a sinner or a saint. I saw something worse, someone invisible. A shadow with tired eyes and cracked lips. Someone who wasn't dramatic enough to be saved or quiet enough to be ignored. Someone whose pain didn't fit in parables.
I slid down to the tiles of the shower, the cold of the porcelain grounding me just enough to stay upright. My whole body ached with that quiet desperation only addicts understand, the kind that doesn't scream for more, but begs for less. Less noise, less memory, less of everything.
I laid out six thick lines in a row, not because I was reckless, but because I was exhausted. My fingers moved slowly, almost tenderly, as if the ritual deserved reverence. I told myself it was just enough to take the edge off. Just enough to slow the racing thoughts, to soften the ache in my chest, to silence the memory of that someone I used to be. Just enough to maybe take a nap and not wake up in that feeling again.
When the last line was gone, I tried to stand, maybe to clean up, maybe to return to the living room and act like I hadn't just tried to vanish. But my knees buckled before I could decide. I reached for the wall, missed it completely, and collapsed with the quiet elegance of someone used to falling without being caught.
There was no pain. No grand moment. No flashing lights or poetic last breath. Just a sudden and suffocating stillness. My thoughts faded in surrender. Like a curtain falling in an empty theatre. I didn't dream. I didn't float. I didn't see God or light or my childhood from a

distance. There was no slideshow. No great release. Only absence. As if I had been carefully lifted out of the world and placed nowhere at all. I wasn't scared. I just wasn't there.

–

I woke up in the hospital, again. My muscles were shaking from the cramps. Bella was beside me, her fingers wrapped gently around mine, like she was still trying to hold me here, in the world. When we got home, I lay in the living room with Bella and Sarah, sharing chips and half-hearted laughter. The kind of moment that pretends to be ordinary, but only because the situation hadn't yet settled into anyone's bones.
And then Jaco and Lina emerged.
He didn't say *are you okay?* or *thank God you're alive.* He looked down at me, barely recovered from nearly dying, and asked:
"What are we going to do about the door?"
Bella and I looked at each other.
They weren't trying to hurt me. That's what I keep telling myself. But they were affirming what I already feared was true; that I was nothing but a disruption. That my pain was more inconvenient than it was real.

Later, Sarah and Kim told me what happened while I was unconscious. They said I'd been in the bathroom too long. That they heard me gasping. Matty kicked in the door, splitting the wood and leaving a gaping hole. I had been on the floor, foaming, my eyes wide open and then slowly closing. Sarah called 911 while Kim knelt beside me, following live instructions from a paramedic over the phone. Sarah even showed the operator a live video of my body on the floor. And through it all, Matty screamed in divine tongues — loud, unintelligible declarations that made the chaos almost surreal. Nothing like a man screaming heavenly gibberish over your unconscious body to remind you that salvation's a group effort. A *loud*, uncoordinated, deeply unhelpful group effort.

There I was: overdosing on my bathroom floor, while a man summoned the heavens in a language I barely trusted, while the girl I used to play football with took turns trying not to cry loud enough to make it worse.

The door broke. Yes. It splintered under the force of someone trying to save me.

Maybe we *should* have held a funeral for the door. I considered writing an obituary: *Survived countless slams, passive-aggressive closings, and one failed DIY hinge repair. Died trying to save someone no one else wanted to touch.*

The door broke clean. It broke at the right time, for the right reason, and no one questioned its worth afterward. I didn't. It got repaired, and I got whispered about.

Apparently, the door was the only thing worth mourning. What I don't understand, and maybe never will, is how the main message of Christianity is to love the broken, to sit with the lepers, to eat with the tax collectors, and yet here I was, treated as if my soul was contagious.

If grace was contagious, they would've caught it too. But it turns out, fear has a stronger immune system.

Where is the love for the poor in spirit, when the spirit is buried under dope and shame? Where is mercy, when mercy needs a reason to show up?

That's the thing about conditional love; it always looks generous, until you fail the terms and realize it was just tolerance dressed up in scripture. They always say it's about your personal relationship with God. That the church is just a flawed vessel, "cracked but well-meaning", and you shouldn't let imperfect people poison perfect faith. But that relationship was never meant to be lived alone. It's supposed to be carried in communion, anchored in fellowship, not whispered into a void and called enough. And when the body of Christ starts rejecting its own limbs, when mercy can't make it past the church hallway, you start to wonder if the vessel was cracked, or hollow. Maybe that's what broke me the most: being told God loved me unconditionally by people who clearly didn't.

And still, somehow, I kept trying to earn it anyway.

I was still me. Still the girl who handed out offering baskets in Jaco's team at church. Still the friend who helped Lina pronounce irregular verbs in French. Still the girl who once believed so hard it burned holes in her chest.

But now, because I was actively ruining myself, I was none of that to them.

I was a walking void. A body carrying all the discomfort they didn't want to hold. A reflection they couldn't bear to see themselves in.

And that, more than any antidote they could've rushed into my veins, brought breath back into a body that had already given up. Not that there's a real antidote for cocaine. You can't reverse it; you can only ride it out if your body lets you. But judgment? That shit's fast-acting and lethal. No antidote for that. Because sometimes, what revives you isn't medicine, but the way someone looks at you and sees a future instead of a failure.

I didn't know it yet, but love, the real kind, doesn't knock. It breaks the door, pulls up a chair, and stays. Somewhere between the silence and the sirens, between the shattered doorframe and Bella's hand in mine, it had already begun.

PART 11

THE GOSPEL ACCORDING TO LISBETH

Chapter 1

Bella knew before I did, that her role in my life had changed. It wasn't a fight. There were no words.

When I moved into Lisbeth and Michael's home, Bella and I didn't speak for almost a month. But we were still good. Still us. Like the silence was a gentle agreement between two people who had carried too much. She was breaking too, just differently, in the way people do when they're handed the role of savior before they've figured out how to save themselves.

There comes a point where witnessing someone else's suffering becomes its own form of violence. Especially when it's wrapped in love.

I was still breathing, still waking up, still putting one foot in front of the other. But she knew that wasn't the same as living. And the truth is, it's not your job to drag your best friend's body back from the brink every time they try to vanish. Not forever. She'd done more than most. She'd held me through withdrawals and wordless sobbing, through fevered nights, foetal-position mornings, and suicide attempts. So, when she handed me over to Lisbeth, it wasn't abandonment.

It was the highest act of trust.

She chose to live, and to let me try. I welcomed it. The

shift. The help. The change. Not because I believed in recovery, but because I had stopped believing in anything else. By then, I didn't feel breakable, just used up. Like the damage had already been done, and anything that came next would just be white noise.

–

I didn't ask for the memory. It arrived on a quiet morning, while Michael was outside whistling to the birds and Lisbeth was making coffee, her voice gently humming along to some Danish radio tune. The smell of toasted rye bread filled the air like normalcy had roots here. And yet, my body remembered. Before I did. It always did.

It started with a cigarette run. That's what we called it. Another friend — not Bella — was ten years older than me, but we were orbiting the same slow implosion, so age didn't matter. One night, we were hanging out at her place, the way we always did, two broken people trying to look normal, flicking ash and pretending we had somewhere to be. Later, we stepped out to go to the corner store to get more cigarettes. But she veered toward a taxi by the train station, casual like it was nothing, and I followed. Because I always did. Even when everything in me whispered that I shouldn't.

Like I always did. Even when every nerve in me whispered: not this street, not tonight.

Istedgade in Copenhagen is known for what it hides in plain sight; addiction, prostitution, ghosts still walking in skin. We ended up near H17, the injection centre, where those still clinging to the edge could shoot up with clean needles and supervision, a place that claimed to offer safety in a world that had none.

Outside were bodies that had already left, eyes that blinked but didn't see, laughter that sounded like it was echoing from the bottom of a grave. We used. Fast. Desperately. Ran out even faster. And so began the kind of night you only understand once it's too late to leave. A loop of searching, nodding, chasing smoke you can never hold.

There was a man named Moses. Sweet, deep-eyed, and full of unexpected softness. We spoke about life like we were old friends, and for a moment, I thought maybe this night wouldn't break me the way I thought it would. But addiction's mask is made of wax; all warmth until it melts. When Moses lit the pipe, he changed. His voice lifted into a manic song, my name echoing loudly down the street, his limbs jittering, the light gone from his gaze like someone had shut off the soul inside.

And then there was the Moroccan man. Older. Hungrier. He had a thing for me. And I had a thing for self-destruction disguised as strategy. I used his interest to get more drugs, each line a silent agreement I didn't want to make. I pulled away if he got touchy, laughed it off, played the broken girl card like it was armour. But monsters don't need consent. They only need opportunity.

We sat on a bench outside H17, my friend lost in another conversation, and him — too close, too quiet. I felt a curtain fall between me and the world, like I was watching my body from outside it. That's what addiction does. It teaches you how to dislocate your spirit from your skin.

Then suddenly, his hands were on me, pushing my head down toward his exposed crotch like it was owed. I pulled back, fast, a whisper sharp with panic, "That's not what I want from you." He apologized, theatrically, then wrapped his arms around me in a way that didn't feel like regret but ownership.

He lifted me like I weighed nothing. And maybe I didn't. I was all bones and bargaining at that point.
He started walking toward an alley.
Morning had begun to stretch its pale fingers across the sky, but everything still felt like night. I froze. Every part of me said: don't speak, don't resist. He'd been volatile all evening, and I could feel violence resting just under the surface, waiting for a reason.
He had already tried to steer me toward that alley twice, each time a little more insistent, like he thought the night would eventually obey him. But my friend ran after us. She grabbed me, yanked me back like she was pulling a child out of traffic. We left.
Later, he came looking for me again. Outside my friend's apartment, calling up to the window, offering free drugs and promises of travel, asking to see me "just for a second." I hid in the bedroom, heart in my throat, while Bella and my friend smoked by the window and told him to leave. And he did. But not fast enough to take his face from my memory.
That night broke something in Bella. The weight of witnessing two people she loved implode under the same roof was too much. I didn't blame her. There's only so long you can be the thread holding someone else together before you start fraying yourself. She didn't walk away in anger; she let go in love.
I curled into her that night like a child. Sobbed into her chest, foetal, inconsolable. She held me like it was the last time, and maybe it was, for now. That kind of holding changes shape when survival becomes a solo act.
Soon after, Lisbeth came to pick me up, it was a quiet transition. From one lifeline to the next. From a friend who was drowning beside me to a woman who could swim and had a raft.

Lisbeth is Bella's aunt.

But that's such a sterile title for someone whose voice feels like a balm and whose eyes don't flinch at the worst parts of you. When we first met, she was calm in a way that unnerved me. Beautiful, too — that kind of beauty you don't expect in someone who looks at you like a case file but makes you feel like a daughter.

Blue eyes, skin tanned by decades of doing the hard things, straight to the point in a way that felt like fresh air. Like there was no time to pretend anymore. And I didn't want to pretend either.

Her husband Michael, on the other hand, was made of joy and Danish garden soil. A police officer with the enthusiasm of a golden retriever and the bluntness of a philosopher who forgot he wasn't at a dinner party. "How can someone as smart as you make such dumb decisions?" he asked once while sipping coffee. Dead serious. No judgment, just confusion. I didn't know how to answer, but I liked that he asked.

I moved into their camper in the garden. The silence there was so loud I could hear my heartbeat. And birds. I didn't know I liked birds until then. Every morning, they sang like it was safe to wake up.

Michael would make coffee, Lisbeth would head to work, and I'd stay back, my body collapsing from all the calm. After a year of chaos, my nervous system was no longer buzzing, it was grieving; for what I'd endured, what I never had, the version of me that didn't have to perform to be protected.

The first few weeks, I mostly slept or stayed alone. The hallucinations hadn't stopped — coke takes a long time to leave the body when you've been using like it's water. I remember one night waking up to a giant spider crawling on me, in the camper. I panicked, swatted the air, saw it multiply, ran into the living room and found Michael. He didn't say much, just used his voice like a lighthouse. I wanted to believe his voice could guide me home, but I wasn't sure I had a coastline left.

Probably just shipwrecks. And hallucinated spiders.
The thing about withdrawal; it doesn't always look like shaking or screaming; sometimes, it's hallucinating arachnids and needing someone to believe you long enough for the monsters to leave.

Michael once started talking about Van Gogh, not like he was reciting facts, but like he was remembering a friend who had once saved his life. There was something about the way he spoke — not casually, not academically, but with this wild, reverent fire — that made me pause. I knew the name, sure. I knew the sunflowers, the ear, the madness. But I didn't know the story the way Michael told it: as if pain had a brushstroke, as if loneliness could make colours sing. His voice trembled a little when he spoke of the letters Van Gogh wrote to his brother Theo, how he longed to be understood, how he kept painting even as the world mistook his devotion for dysfunction. And I was deeply moved. I understood.
That night, I googled him. I started reading about his breakdowns, the psychiatric hospital, the poverty, the hunger, the hallucinations, the unbearable ache of wanting to be seen without having to perform to earn it. I scrolled through his work, not with an art critic's eye, but with the hunger of someone trying to find a mirror. And I did. It was all there: the bruised colour palettes, the violent skies, the quiet madness stitched into every line. I saw myself in the textures, in the imbalance, in the quiet pleading underneath all that beauty. I thought, this is what it means to survive in public while dying in private. And maybe Michael didn't say it that way, but I felt it. His passion for Van Gogh didn't just make me feel safer, it made me want to stay. And that confused me. Not the safety part, I'd started to crave that in small, secret ways, but the way Michael spoke about someone so broken with such reverence. Like Van Gogh's suffering wasn't just a tragedy, but something sacred. His voice trembled

when he talked about loneliness, the letters, the hunger, the desperate need to be understood. It wasn't pity. It was something else. A kind of fierce tenderness that didn't look away. I didn't understand how someone could care that deeply about a man who'd spiraled so far, who'd lost so much, who hadn't been saved in the end. It made me wonder what Michael would see if he looked at me the same way; if he'd find poetry in the wreckage, or just a warning sign that people passed on the road without slowing down. I wanted to pull away from it, because that kind of attention scared me more than judgment ever had. But I stayed. Because if someone like Van Gogh could be remembered for more than his chaos, maybe I could too.

The next day, Lisbeth didn't ask questions. She just said, "Get in the car." We drove to an art supply store, one of those cozy little places that smell like dust and potential, and she bought me paints and canvases like it was the most natural thing in the world. No speech. No therapeutic framing. Just a woman who'd seen something flicker in me and decided to feed it before it went out.

That night, I painted, not because I knew how, but because I had to. There was no sketch, no plan, just colour poured from whatever lived under my skin, like bleeding without the blood, like if I didn't get it out, the silence might kill me. I stayed up until the sun began to peel back the dark, the garden waking up behind the camper, and for once, I didn't dread waking up, because the canvas was waiting for me to paint what I felt. I wanted to show Michael. I wanted to thank him, even if I didn't have the words.

And when he saw it; just shapes and grief and a storm that didn't know how to end, he nodded, slowly, like he recognized it. Like maybe he'd painted it once too, just in different colours.

My nightmares were worse. In them, I'd walk through

sandy alleys in some war-torn dreamscape, find a toddler's decapitated head, get chased by machete-wielding silhouettes who warned, "If anyone speaks another language, we kill them." I would wake up sweating, chest caving in, and go about my day like that was normal. Because for me, it was. I didn't know trauma could live in dreams. Nobody teaches you that. Nobody tells you how violence stored in the body rewrites your REM cycle, or that your brain will try to warn you, not with words, but with war zones stitched into your sleep.
I'd go inside and talk to Lisbeth. We didn't discuss the nightmares directly. She just looked at me long enough, and I'd start talking about other things. Family. Power dynamics. Control disguised as care. We'd talk about "how things should be," which was really code for what we never had. She gave me her time and her brain and her space. Sometimes I'd forget she was trying to keep a professional distance, because somewhere between the tea and the jokes and the way she looked at me like I could do this, she became more than a teacher. And when she told me about her past; the pain, the pills, the quiet breakdowns nobody saw coming; I realized I wasn't a lost cause to her. I was just a girl in a process.
Michael didn't do boundaries; he did loyalty, loud opinions, and hugs so big you forgot you weren't family. His optimism was so intense it bordered on delusion, but the kind you want to believe in when your own reality has teeth.
He didn't get it all, but he didn't pretend to. That's what I needed.

And then there was Camilla Johnson.

Lisbeth had gathered a meeting at her mother's house to figure out how the hell to help me.
Camilla came — the founder of an organization called "Inside Out", she was the kind of woman who walked out

of hell still smoking.
She talked fast, laughed loudly, and had a fury for injustice that didn't need an audience to stay lit.
As she spoke about sects; the quiet mechanisms, the brainwashing dressed in scripture, the way they bait the broken... something clicked in me. Not because she said, "The Last Reformation is a sect", but because she didn't have to.
They checked every box.
And it made me sick.
That night I scrolled through old texts from Tom. "How's Copenhagen? Are you hanging out with the right people?" "I'm doing a TV interview... would love if you could share your story." Your story. As if he owned it. As if my trauma was just marketing content.
I had been in a sect. I didn't say it out loud for days. Letting that truth land felt like watching a bridge collapse after you've already crossed it; safe but shaking.
The church had failed me again. I had asked Horizon if they could help finance rehab. Their answer was vague and polite. "We'll pray. We'll see." The next Sunday they hosted a service with massive stage props and booming sound systems, as if Jesus had a lighting technician and a fog machine. No, the glory of God apparently doesn't extend to addicts who don't tithe.
Lisbeth and Michael didn't have a million kroner. But they had a spare camper, a fridge, a willingness to try, and a kind of love that doesn't need an audience. They never told me I was chosen, they just treated me like I belonged. All this kindness. I didn't know what to do with it. My body scanned every gesture like it was a trap, because it always had been.
I kept waiting for a bill, a condition or a catch.
And when none came, I started to feel guilty.

Like I was stealing from people who didn't realize they were being robbed.

Lisbeth would tell me to rest. Michael would say he was proud. And I would smile like I believed them, then go cry in the camper because nothing in my body knew how to digest grace.

But it changed everything.

Chapter 2

I was later referred to psychiatry, the F-ACT team. Flexible Assertive Community Treatment. A model for people like me who weren't just struggling but unravelling. Pia, a nurse there, listened like listening could change the world. She put me on antidepressants. They helped level the spikes in emotion I used to medicate with pills and powder.

But when I brought up my food issues; the restricting, the obsessive rituals, the weight loss, I was told it wasn't "severe enough." Never mind the BMI. Never mind that I was cooking meals for others, tasting a single salted spoonful, then spitting it into the trash like it was poison.

In Denmark, unless you're collapsing, you're coping.

The earlier you treat an eating disorder, the better the odds of recovery, but that's not how the system works. And so, you fade. Quietly. Elegantly. Until you're no longer a priority, but a tragedy.

I often wonder how my mother would see all this; the therapy, the medication, the vulnerability scribbled into medical charts. In her world, you didn't speak of such things. You prayed. You screamed. You swallowed pain and called it strength.

Anything else was indulgent, selfish and dangerous.

For years, I wore that shame like a badge, believing I'd

failed by needing help, by putting my pain into words instead of silence. To admit I was unwell felt like becoming the very thing she warned me about: dramatic, unstable, broken beyond repair.

But I've learned something softer, something steadier than rebellion: It isn't weak to fall apart. It isn't shameful to need structure when your mind has been shaped by chaos. Psychiatry isn't a crutch; it's a language, and for those of us raised in screaming, chaos, in homes where silence only followed the slam of a door, psychiatry becomes the first translation of the pain no one ever paused long enough to name. Seeking help isn't surrender. It's a quiet way of saying: *I still believe there's something in me worth saving. Even if that something isn't obvious to me, maybe it is to someone else.*

In the world I come from, believing you're worth saving is an act of quiet rebellion. And even then, no guarantees.

But I had Lisbeth. And Michael. And Camilla. And a quiet place to wake up where birds sang, and silence didn't mean danger, and nobody screamed behind closed doors. Bella had laid the foundation. Lisbeth and Michael gave it walls. Just... walls. With art. With warmth. And Michael, feeding birds like he was stitching the sky back together. He'd stand in the garden, scattering seeds with a reverence that felt almost sacred, then gesture for me to come watch.

"You see those?" he'd say, pointing to a mess of flapping wings. "Those fly in groups. They take turns leading. When one gets tired, another takes the front."

I stood there, heartbroken in places I hadn't mapped yet, and nodded like I understood, but it landed anyway.

The idea that survival didn't have to be a solo flight.

That someone could step in when your wings gave out, not out of pity, but out of pattern, nature and instinct.

He went on, talking about migration and moulting seasons, and I half-listened, half-sank into the softness of it all.
Because I'd spent so long fighting winds alone that the thought of formation flying felt like a fairytale.
Michael didn't know he was explaining safety.
He thought he was just talking about birds.
But that's how love sneaks in.
Through birdseeds. Through coffee steam.
Through a man who thinks watching sparrows share sky is the best part of the day.
And I believed him, because when someone shows you that even birds rest,
you start to wonder if maybe you can too.

Lisbeth let me cook for them like it was the most natural thing in the world, and not even as a reward, not as rehabilitation, but as an invitation. She didn't frame it as a lesson or a milestone; she simply handed me the kitchen like someone placing a letter into trusted hands, knowing I'd decide what to do with it. There were no instructions, just permission, quiet and clean, like the air that moved through her home when the windows were open.
The first time I peeled potatoes in her kitchen, Michael was outside, whistling in the garden, some half-melody I didn't recognize, but that rose and fell like a bird that wasn't quite sure where it was flying, only that it had always been safe to return here. He was probably feeding the sparrows, murmuring something about how some birds fly in groups while others learn to navigate storms alone, like it was both a fact and a prayer. And inside, I moved through the space as though I'd always belonged in it, like I hadn't just come from lost battles, like the kitchen didn't know what my hands had trembled through.
But this was the kind of house where silence didn't mean

tension, and where the hum of a stovetop and the occasional gust of wind through the open garden door said more than any sermon. Where a man could whistle outside, and a woman could trust an addict to cook dinner, and neither needed it to be anything more than what it was: ordinary, which is to say, holy.

I cooked slowly, with the tenderness of someone relearning the shape of their own hands. There was no pressure to get it perfect. No one hovering or watching me for signs of collapse. Just Lisbeth setting the table like it was any other evening, Michael whistling something shapeless in the distance, and me, slicing garlic, flipping chicken, tasting sauces, trying not to spit them out from old instinct.

And when I brought the food to the table, Lisbeth didn't perform gratitude; she just looked at me like she'd always known I could do this, even when I hadn't. And when Michael took the first bite, he smiled like it was confirmation of something he'd never doubted. It didn't heal me, but it anchored me. Like building something stable, one spoonful at a time.

Some houses hand you rules, but Lisbeth's handed me oil and a frying pan.

Some men bark advice through a closed window, Michael just whistled in the garden, like he knew that healing doesn't always show up in therapy rooms.

Sometimes it smells like rosemary and sounds like a man talking to birds.

Sometimes, love looks like a camper in the garden and silence that doesn't bite.

Sometimes, it looks like being handed a second chance by people who didn't owe you anything and gave you everything anyway.

And sometimes, that's how healing begins, not with grand gestures or perfect plans, but with sparrows in formation, a frying pan in your hand, someone that stays just long enough to keep the boat from tipping.

Chapter 3

I didn't get diagnosed with anorexia until there was someone else inside me; someone the system decided was worth protecting. Not because the symptoms weren't there before, they were. I had spent years perfecting the art of starvation, dressing it up as discipline. I treated food like a currency I couldn't afford, like a luxury meant for those who didn't carry war zones in their bloodstream. But it wasn't until there were two heartbeats in my body that someone finally called it what it was: anorexia, tangled up with PTSD like barbed wire around a hunger strike. Turns out, your body only matters once it becomes someone else's home.

Before that, my restriction was a quirky footnote. "A bit of stress", they said. "A stubborn phase". As if skipping meals was a teenage rebellion, not a coping strategy with calorie counts. Never mind the night sweats, the hypervigilance, the auditory hallucinations of ambulance sirens or the flashbacks that made me clamp my ears and rock like a child in distress. Never mind the hours spent weighing food and calculating safety in spoons. I was surviving, right? Surviving like a haunted house; upright, but not exactly safe to enter. And in Denmark, if you're vertical and vaguely employed, you're considered functional.

If you're not bleeding out, you're "managing." And if

you're not managing, well, are you sure?
But now, with a pregnancy to protect, the narrative changed. Suddenly my thinness wasn't "concerning", it was dangerous. Suddenly, I wasn't just a struggling woman with trust issues and a stubborn appetite; I was a risk to an unborn life. And the system cares about unborn lives more than the broken ones still walking around, apparently.
And that's the tragedy: if I hadn't gotten pregnant, I probably still wouldn't be getting the right help. Even my psychologist in Team 3 said it — directly, with eyes that didn't blink away from mine: "The system failed you. And it fails people like you all the time."
It wasn't her fault. These professionals were the lights in a system that runs mostly on motion sensors and budget cuts. But that diagnosis only came because someone else was at stake. It took a second heartbeat to make mine matter.
And that still makes me sick.
I don't blame her. She was the good part of the system. She was the part that wanted to fix the cracks, not just chart them, but her power stopped at the clipboard. And clipboards don't stop girls from dying. They just keep track of the descent.

And I couldn't shake the thought: If I hadn't gotten pregnant, would I still be slipping through?
Because food was never the enemy, reality was. And hunger gave me something to master; it was about control, or the illusion of it when my nervous system was hijacked by trauma I didn't know how to name. It was a mute button on the screaming and a quiet war I could win every day just by saying no to my own body.
Eating meant letting the trauma move through. Restricting meant pressing pause.
But when I saw that ultrasound photo; that tiny, stubborn person, I felt something powerful shift.

For the first time, feeding myself became about more than just surviving, it became about not passing down what I never got.
I didn't want this baby to inherit my fluency in self-erasure.
And yet, how cruel — how fucking cruel — that the only reason I was finally being treated like a person worth saving was because I was carrying someone else. That my worth was only declared urgent when someone else might bleed for it.
I was no longer a girl with bad coping mechanisms.
I was a vessel.
A container. A courier.
A maybe-mother with a track record.
And that changed everything... but it shouldn't have had to.

I kept that ultrasound photo.
Not as a token of sentimentality, but because it proved I was real, that something was growing where, for years, I thought nothing could survive. Like a dandelion pushing through concrete, whispering: *Not everything inside you is dead.*
I stared at it that night. I laid it on the desk in the corner of my tiny 14m² room in Måløv, the kind of room that feels too small for your thoughts when they're loud. Outside, streetlights hummed like tired angels, casting the same orange glow I once mistook for safety when I was a teenager on the run.
I'd been so certain I would never be a mother, not because I didn't want to love, but because I thought I might be genetically wired to destroy.
My mother never thought there was anything wrong with the way she raised me, and maybe that was the most terrifying part; that you could cause so much harm and still sleep at night. Still braid your daughter's hair before telling her she was the reason God might

withhold grace.

I was afraid I would wake up one day and hear her voice in my mouth.

But something changed in that hospital room. When I held that picture — that accidental, maybe-not-so-accidental ultrasound image left by the nurse — I didn't see a mistake.
I saw someone I hadn't met yet, who already felt familiar. And then, out of nowhere, something ancient and primal took over. It wasn't logical. It wasn't even maternal. It was a kind of sacred rage. A promise.
A vow etched in marrow: I will protect you, even from the parts of me that never got the chance to heal.
You will not inherit my ghosts.
You will not learn love by fearing it.
You will be safe with me, I promise.
And I meant it. I meant it with every cell in my exhausted, chemically bruised, half-nourished body.
I meant it like a prayer screamed through a keyhole.
I meant it when I tore up the appointment slip for the abortion.
When I walked back into the waiting room and told Nick, flatly, that they had given me a date, I couldn't say more. I needed time to process what had just happened, to hold space for the version of myself who never thought she'd survive, let alone raise someone else.
He didn't ask questions. Just looked at me like I was a stranger. And maybe I was.
Maybe that was the first moment I became someone I hadn't met yet either.
The air still smelled like hospital, like bleach and broken promises, but something inside my chest cracked open, not into a wound, but into a doorway. Through it, I could see her. Not an idea. Not a symptom. Her. Diana. Not yet named. Not yet born.

But already rewriting what I thought was inevitable.

The moment that second pink line ghosted its way onto the plastic stick, she was in the room, blinking like maybe her vision had short-circuited. I looked at her. She looked at me. And then I ran. Not metaphorically. I physically ran around the apartment with the pregnancy test still in my hand, like it was a lit firecracker and not a piece of moulded plastic declaring that my uterus had found a tenant.

She followed, slowly, the way you approach a feral cat with a sprained paw.

"Okay," Bella said. Just that. "Okay. We'll figure it out."

My whole nervous system exhaled for the first time in years. It never even crossed my mind to hide it from her, or from Lisbeth, or Michael, or even Pia at the F-ACT clinic. Maybe because for the first time, there was nothing shameful about what was growing in me. The shame had already been wrung out by years of overdoses, self-hatred, and late-night near misses with death. What was left now was just truth; uneasy, inconvenient, miraculous truth.

When Pia found out, she didn't smile. Not in that patronizing "oh, a baby will save you" kind of way. She furrowed her brow like she was already running through systems, barriers and protocol. That kind of care is rare. So, when she fast-tracked a referral to the eating disorder team — not because my BMI had finally made the cut, but because I was pregnant — it landed with a thud in my gut.

Referral to Team 3. Severe Eating Disorders.

"Oh," I thought. "So now I qualify."

It felt like a cosmic joke. I'd been restricting my food for years, cooking for others while eating nothing, taste-testing like a chef in a hostage situation, my body was a battlefield, and no one sent reinforcements until there was a baby living in the trenches.

That's when I was finally diagnosed. Anorexia. PTSD.
It wasn't control. It was anaesthesia.
An exorcism by starvation. It had been a way to mute the noise, the nightmares, the flashbacks, and the weight of existing in a body that had been violated, watched, ignored, misunderstood. I wasn't trying to be thin. I was trying to disappear quietly, in a way that didn't alarm anyone.

The first body in my bloodline that decided to shelter, not shatter, because this wasn't a story about a baby saving me; it was about what happens when a woman, whose trauma has taught her to vanish from her own life, finally chooses to stay — even when every cell is begging her to flee, even when the shape of the future is terrifying because no one ever taught her how to hold something fragile without crushing it.

I never wanted children. And the fear wasn't just abstract; it was rooted in muscle memory. My nervous system had been wired for war. I read silence as rejection, mistook love for surveillance and stability for a trap. So, the idea of becoming someone's mother felt like being handed a porcelain doll while your hands are still covered in blood.
Bella knew. She saw it all before I could say it. She always did. I don't remember exactly where we were when she said it.
It wasn't one of those capital-M moments. There was no dramatic music, no warm lighting, no journal entry. Just a pause in the middle of regular life, maybe we were folding laundry, maybe she was making coffee, maybe I was picking at my cuticles again, when Bella looked up and said, with that crooked smile she always used to soften the truth:
"When we realised you were pregnant, I thought in my head: that bitch... she just got clean."

And I laughed, because that's exactly how we talk, irreverent and disarming, like humour was the only language that could hold the weight without breaking. But underneath it, there was a tremor. A plea. *Please don't fall apart again. Not now.*

Everyone around me was quietly bracing for collapse. They didn't say it, not directly, but the fear lived in their bodies. They knew that if I chose not to keep it, there was a very real chance I wouldn't survive the grief. Not because I wanted a baby, but because I didn't know if I could live through another loss that *I* had signed off on.

They were scared — *we* were scared — that if I terminated the pregnancy, I wouldn't come back, that the grief would swallow me whole and spit out the ghost version I'd spent years trying to bury.

It wasn't about morality, or politics. It was survival.

Because I wasn't someone who bounced back from pain; I inhaled it, sat with it, named it mine.

But the decision still felt impossible, because I was being asked to protect something when no one had ever protected me.

To believe in a future I had never seen modelled.

To feed a body growing inside mine when I still forgot to feed myself.

To become a mother when I had spent my entire life being motherless, even when she was in the room.

And yet.

When I saw her on that ultrasound, blurry and utterly unaware of the storm she'd floated into, it wasn't a clean epiphany. It didn't feel like joy or magic. It felt less like saving myself, and more like refusing to leave her behind in the ruins.

To build something; not in spite of what had been lost, but because of it.

I couldn't yet picture her face. But I could already feel the weight of her not existing, and it was unbearable.

So, I chose her. In a way, I chose both of us.

I hadn't picked a name yet. I didn't even know if I would. But sometime around then — maybe the same week, maybe the same hour — I stumbled across that old interview with Lady Diana. The one where she says she never wanted to be the queen of this country, but the queen of people's hearts, in people's hearts.

And it wasn't just the words, it was the way she said them, like every syllable had been carved out of disappointment and defiance, and she still chose to love anyway. Her eyes didn't flinch, and her voice didn't plead. She wasn't performing. She was promising something.

That was the kind of love I had always believed in, even when it felt like fiction, even when it didn't believe in me back. It was the blueprint I kept reaching for in the dark, the one I used to burn down everything that wasn't it.

So, when I heard her say it: *"I don't want to be the queen of this country. I want to be the queen of people's hearts"* — with that quiet, sacred certainty, it wasn't just the words that stayed with me, but the way she looked at the journalist while saying them; steady and unapologetic. Like she wasn't seeking approval, and that gaze — direct, unflinching, heartbreakingly human — said everything I'd ever wanted love to be.

And maybe that's what wrecked me.

Because I knew that love. I'd been waiting for it since I was small enough to believe it had to exist, that there was a kind of love that didn't punish, didn't humiliate, didn't disappear when you needed it most. My whole life had been a rebellion against anything that wasn't that.

So, when she said it, and looked at him like that, I didn't even need to write it down.

It wasn't a decision. It was recognition. My daughter's name would be Diana.

Not after royalty, but after a woman who knew what it meant to be adored and still feel abandoned. Someone

who chose heart over crown. It wasn't a name; it was a promise.
Maybe I wasn't just a vessel.

Maybe I was the first in a long line of trembling hands who didn't pass it on, and not because I was brave, but because something in me paused long enough to wonder what might happen if I didn't flinch this time.
I didn't feel strong. I felt like a loose wire. Like a door someone forgot to lock. But I stayed. In the mess. In the noise no one else could hear. I stayed even when every instinct told me to fold myself small and forget this ever happened.
Because that's the truth no one says out loud: breaking a cycle doesn't feel like healing, it feels like disobedience, trespassing and waking up in someone else's life with no map and no promise.
It means grieving things you were never allowed to name, feeling things your family never had time for, relearning how to breathe without checking the room first.

It is slow, clumsy, ugly at times, but it's real.

And somewhere between the fear and the unfamiliar quiet, I started to realize that maybe this is how it begins. Not with clarity or relief, just the terrifying act of *staying* without a reason, without a reward, only the quiet defiance of remaining long enough to feel the bruises no one else could see begin to heal.

PART 12

SHE'LL REIGN WHERE I CRAWLED

Chapter 1

She will never bow to the things that broke me.

The strange thing is, by the time I started believing I could be a mother, I was already mothering. I was working through a nanny agency in Copenhagen, taking care of a Danish actress's baby, and without knowing it, I was being watched, not in the threatening way I'd grown used to, but in the rare, reverent way someone watches you when they see something good and still, and worth protecting. The way I held the baby, how I slowed down to speak softly, eye-to-eye, how I prepared bottles with a kind of nervous devotion, as if it mattered — because it did — all of it began to ripple outward.
One day my boss called, her voice practically glowing through the phone. "Luna... you won't believe who wants your services." The actress, it turned out, had told her friend — a well-known Danish pop star — about me, and this singer wanted me to care for her child. "She's willing to pay for your travel," my boss said. "It's a longer commute, but she specifically asked for you." I had no

idea who she was; just that, apparently, everyone else did. But something about the request touched me in a place I hadn't realized was still tender, the place that longed to be chosen; not out of pity, not because I was resilient or tragic or "inspiring," but simply because the way I loved made people feel safe.

I said yes.

I worked throughout my pregnancy.

She'd sometimes call me at six in the morning, and I'd come, taking a bus, sometimes biking ten kilometres back and forth through Copenhagen's cold with a belly that grew heavier and a heart that — slowly — began to believe I was capable. I still don't know how I did it, not with the exhaustion, not with the weight of everything I was still carrying from before, but I did it anyway. And caring for their children while waiting for my own became a quiet kind of proof: that I was already becoming what I never thought I could be.

At home, Lisbeth and Michael were already calling themselves *Mormor* and *Morfar*, not as a joke, not as a maybe, but as if the child growing inside me had always belonged to their future. They had claimed us both before I even realized we'd been offered a place to land.

And Bella — Bella was something else entirely. I asked her one day, not formally, not with any big speech, if she wanted to be Diana's godmother, and her eyes filled so quickly with tears that I couldn't tell where the yes began and the knowing ended. It didn't feel like a request, and it didn't feel like an honor. It felt like a continuation of something that had already been written — a deepening, not a decision. She immediately started planning all the things she would do with her: the little routines, the ways she'd help with bedtime, the kind of protective role she'd take, not unlike a second parent. It was fierce, loving, slightly absurd, and entirely her.

When I went to visit Nick, Bella came with me. He

looked hollowed out, told me he was still drinking himself to sleep because of me, said it like it was a confession and a weapon all at once. At the end of the visit, he looked at both of us and said, "Good luck." It wasn't sarcastic. It wasn't loving either. Just flat. Empty. And something in Bella shifted. Her godmother heart — already forming, already stretching — seemed to roar open that day. A nest started to build inside her, not just for me, but for Diana. As if, in that moment, whatever hesitation she may have had disappeared, and the space where a father should've been folded into her without question, without performance — like the role had always been hers and the world was just catching up.

But even with all that support, the doubts came in waves. I was doing my part — going to eating disorder treatment, where my PTSD was treated too, because the two were never separate. My restriction had never been about weight or beauty, not really; it was about control, or the illusion of it, in a body that had never truly felt like mine. I wasn't starving to be smaller — I was starving to stay silent. I was starving to survive.

And like any long famine, you start to forget what full feels like, not just in your body, but in your spirit. And the trauma that had taught me how to disappear was the same trauma that had made my nervous system a minefield. So, recovery couldn't be separated into neat categories. It had to be rooted out from every angle, and I was doing the digging, scared as hell but still showing up.

I often wondered if I could keep doing it while being a mother. If I could feel the rise of flashbacks and still meet Diana with steady hands. If I could stay present when my body screamed to leave. If I could be a safe place, not just in intention, but in execution. And then came the hospital scan, week sixteen. Sarah came with me. The doctor, a woman in her fifties with eyes that seemed older than her body, opened my file and scrolled through it; overdose, suicide attempt, CPTSD, anorexia — the pages stacked like a catalogue of my worst moments, curated without context.

She folded her hands, looked at me without a flicker of warmth, and said, "We can still apply for a special abortion, if you wish."

The air went still.

I hadn't mentioned abortion. I had named my baby. I talked to her every night. I had felt her move. I had pictured her first steps, not in fantasy, but in reality; the kind I planned for in grocery stores and bus stops and spare rooms. And this woman, based solely on my past, decided my future was up for discussion. As if anyone had asked her. As if she'd just wandered into the middle of a sacred conversation and thought, *you know what this needs? My unsolicited plot twist.*

Some people would say she was just doing her job. That it was policy. That she was covering bases. But no. That wasn't protocol. That was judgment masquerading as care. That was the assumption that someone like me, with my track record, with my scars, couldn't possibly mother without repeating the cycle. That my pain was hereditary. That trauma leaked. That my child was already infected just by growing inside me.

It wasn't just unethical. It was violence in a white coat.

And for a second, I believed her. Because that's what happens when you've been broken, you begin to assume that everyone else knows better.

Maybe she's right.

Maybe I'm fooling myself.

Maybe Diana doesn't deserve someone like me — someone this wrecked, this unstable, this stitched together from shame.

Who am I to counter a professional opinion? Who am I to insist I'm capable, when everything I've been through says otherwise?

I was still crying over *Grey's Anatomy* episodes like they were personal betrayals and Googling "can you parent with unresolved trauma" like I was prepping for an exam

Shonda Rhimes was grading.

But I didn't say yes. I didn't flinch.
I said no. Firmly. Without hesitation.
Because somewhere beneath the spiral, a deeper voice had already answered, the one that knew I would not let fear decide the fate of my child. I would not deprive Diana of the kind of mother I knew I could be, not perfectly, not easily, but powerfully, intentionally, and with every ounce of softness I had scraped together.
I biked home in the cold, sobbing, the city blurring past like it couldn't look me in the eye. And when I walked in the door, Bella was waiting. She wiped my tears with the back of her hand like she had done a hundred times before, looked at me the way only she could — all heart, no judgment — and said, "You are not your mother. You will never be your mother."
And when I couldn't believe in myself, she let me borrow her belief. "You can rest in my faith," she whispered, again and again. "And Diana, she's lucky. Not because of who you've been, but because of who you're becoming."
I clung to those words like oxygen. And when the doubts returned, as they always did, her voice was the paper bag I breathed into.
The last months of my pregnancy were softer, and stranger. I stopped working and moved in with Bella, into her tiny room in Copenhagen. We slept side by side. We cried over *Grey's Anatomy*. I wept at screensavers of swimming whales — not because I'd ever been especially into animal rights, but because they were beautiful, and slow, and endangered, and I understood that in a way that felt like kinship. I wasn't endangered anymore, but I still flinched like I was. And now I was growing something that didn't have to be.
Diana developed inside the sound of our voices — mine and Bella's — murmuring over dinner, laughing under shared blankets, whispering our fears to each other when

we thought the other was asleep. And sometimes, late at night, I would wake from nightmares of my mother pacing the hallway of my childhood home. I could hear her footsteps in the dream — angry, deliberate — and I knew what was coming. I would feel her hand hit my back before I even turned around, and I would wake gasping, the phantom sting still alive in my skin.

But the difference was — this time, I wasn't waking up alone.

This time, I was not trapped in a house that hated me.

I was safe. In Bella's bed. In her presence. In the nest we were building, not just for Diana, but for ourselves.

There were still ghosts, but they no longer ran the house, and there was still hunger, but now it had a name, and a reason to loosen its grip. The bruises hadn't vanished; they never really do. But for once, I wasn't passing them down. And I began to understand something that changed everything:

This time, the cycle *could* stop.

Not because I was healed, but because I wasn't doing it alone.

For the first time, I wasn't rehearsing my exit, I was learning how to remain in my body, in the moment, in the story.

Not out of clarity.

Not out of certainty.

But because someone *had* to end the echo.

And this time, I chose to become the quiet after the scream.

One heartbeat deciding not to carry the bruises we can't see into another life.

Chapter 2

Nick didn't reach out again after he said, *"Good luck."* I didn't expect him to. There was no suspense, no lingering sense of "maybe." His silence didn't sting; it just confirmed the shape of the absence I had already made room for.

Still, when I found out I was having a girl, I sent him a message. Just a simple one:

Hey Nick, I know you don't want to hear from me, but I just want you to know that the door is always open for you to meet her. Whatever you decide is totally fine. I hope you're doing well. You don't have to answer this message. I just wanted to let you know. —Luna

He didn't answer. Not for weeks.

Then, two months later, his name showed up on my phone again — no greeting, no acknowledgment, no mention of her.

I need your bank information.

That was all.

And that's when it settled; the quiet, conclusive truth of it. He wouldn't be showing up. Not emotionally, not physically, not with stories or Sunday visits or half-efforts wrapped in guilt. Just the practical bare minimum, automated and impersonal.

I knew what I was signing up for. And I understood exactly what he had already signed out of.

As I approached my due date, the room I had been renting was no longer an option. It wasn't personal, just logistical, I couldn't stay there with a newborn. So, I packed up my things in quiet waves, folding my clothes into a suitcase that felt more like a lifeboat than luggage and moved in with Bella full-time.

We didn't know how long it would be. I had applied for an apartment, some godsend of a place where I could begin this next part of my life with a door that locked and a kitchen I didn't share. But two weeks before my due date, there was still no answer.

And let me tell you, when you're eight months pregnant and living out of plastic bags in someone else's home, your body doesn't care that you're technically safe. It just knows there's no nest. And when the body knows there's no nest, it panics. Quietly, usually at 3 a.m., while your best friend is asleep beside you, unaware that you're internally debating whether it's unethical to build a baby corner in someone else's living room.

People talk about the "nesting instinct" like it's adorable. Like pregnant women just wake up one day possessed by the spirit of Marie Kondo and a Pinterest board. But it's not cute. It's primal. It's like your body is screaming *prepare the world or something will die.* I scrubbed things that didn't belong to me. I folded towels like I was preparing for royalty. I reorganized my things in shelves in a way that didn't make sense, all while crying over the fact that my daughter didn't even have a drawer yet, let alone a dresser.

"Luna," Bella would say, like she was reciting some ancient truth, "it's okay. We'll figure it out." She said it every time I panicked, like it was her personal spell against uncertainty.

And maybe it was. Maybe it worked. Because we kept going. Even with no plan. Even with no nursery.

I remember sitting on Bella's bed one night, my belly tight and low, scrolling through listings like they held the answer to something bigger than housing. Two weeks from term, and still no place of our own. No nursery to fold into. No walls to repaint with softness. I wasn't worried Diana would feel unloved. I was worried she'd be born into my chaos before I had the chance to show her the opposite. That the love would be there, but the landing place wouldn't.

But the truth was, I wasn't preparing a space. I was preparing myself. Every sleepless night, every panicked call to boligkontoret, every whispered "we'll figure it out" was the real nesting.

And maybe that's what they don't tell you: sometimes the home doesn't come with walls and a welcome mat.

Sometimes it comes in the shape of two women sleeping side by side, making space in their lives before there's space on paper.

What held me together in those final weeks wasn't strength. It was the quiet scaffolding of the people around me. Anni and Kjeld, my chosen grandparents, showed up in that gentle, consistent way that doesn't make a scene but makes all the difference. Lisbeth and Michael checked in every day, sometimes just with a smile or a short text, as if to say, "You're still seen." And Bella, of course, was everywhere. In the waiting rooms. On the phone. On the other end of a late-night sigh. But even with that web of love around me, something in me was beginning to fray.

By eight months, I was so physically uncomfortable that it was hard to tell where my body ended and the pain began. Diana had discovered my ribcage like it was a kick drum, and her long legs pressed so hard into my pelvis that my sciatic nerve felt like it was lit on fire. I couldn't sleep. Not even in short bursts. Bedtime for me meant party time for her. And the longer the exhaustion dragged on, the more my mental health followed. Hormones, lack of sleep, the ache in my hips, the mounting fear — they all pooled together into a kind of fog I couldn't shake.

I used to think pregnancy was some glowing, mystical state. That's what movies say, isn't it? A warm montage of cravings, glowing skin, and loving belly rubs. But real pregnancy, at least in the last stretch, felt more like a long-haul endurance test you didn't sign up for. No one talks about how claustrophobic it is to live in a body that's no longer just yours, how fragile your mind becomes when you can't move properly, sleep deeply, or cry without feeling like your organs might fall out.

My midwife saw it plainly. She didn't sugarcoat. "You're at your edge," she said. "We'll induce you at week thirty-eight. If your body's this worn down now, it won't have what it needs when labour starts naturally." I nodded, relieved and terrified. It felt like cheating. It also felt like mercy.

Bella came with me to every appointment. And she'd be there for the birth, too. I didn't have to ask. It was already decided in the way she kept track of the questions I always forgot to ask.

In those moments, as the calendar closed in on Diana's arrival, I could feel a strange, aching emptiness settle in beside the anticipation. A longing for the kind of mother I didn't have. Not because she wasn't present, but because her presence had never brought peace.

It's hard to describe the specific kind of grief that shows up when you need a mother and realize yours isn't someone you can turn to. It makes everything feel thinner, exposed and sacred, in a way. Because you must walk through it without the comfort you were supposed to be given and still give comfort to someone new.

One day, I visited Mormor. That's Lisbeth's mother, Bella's grandmother, my chosen grandmother. (The family tree, I know — it's tangled, but it's mine.) She

smiled when she saw me waddle through the door and said, "It would be wonderful if you found a place close to us, to Morfar and me." She listed off a couple of side alleys in the neighbourhood, ones I didn't recognize by name.
A few days later, I got the call: an apartment was available. In one of the exact alleys, she'd wished for. And just like that, the ground beneath me started to feel less like quicksand.

I adored Mormor and Morfar. I still do. Mormor, with her wit and poker face that hides a heart made of honey. Morfar, who might be one of the funniest men alive. We became unlikely best friends. Moving close to them didn't just mean comfort. It meant I could be there for them too, the way they'd been there for me. It felt like building something circular, something that didn't end in loss but started with love.

Diana arrived on February 24th.

The keys to the new apartment wouldn't come until March 1st. So, for that first week, I stayed with Lisbeth's sister — another thread in this chosen family I hadn't asked for but had somehow been given. My newborn daughter slept in my arms in someone else's bedroom, and for the first time in a long time, I didn't feel displaced. I felt held. The apartment itself was empty, no furniture, no crib, no softness. But I didn't even have time to panic. Lisbeth and Michael showed up. Mormor rallied the family. Everything I needed appeared, piece by piece, before I even asked. No one waited for me to collapse. They just acted.
That kind of love still stuns me.
Because it's the opposite of how I grew up, where asking was dangerous and needing meant weakness. Here, needing was allowed. It wasn't punished. It was

anticipated. And that's something I hope Diana never has to unlearn; that being cared for doesn't have to come with a cost.

One afternoon, a few days after we'd settled in, Mormor showed up unannounced, opening the door the same way I do when I visit her: no knock, just presence. She had a lamp in her hand; one I hadn't asked for but clearly needed. Without saying much, she stepped inside, set it down in the corner by the couch, and turned to leave.

"Thank you, Mormor, that's so sweet of you," I said.

She shrugged like it meant nothing, already halfway out the door. "That's not a sacrifice," she replied, dry as ever.

Now, when I help her with something and she says thank you, I shrug and say, "That's not a sacrifice."

And every time, we both crack up, not because it's funny, but because it's ours.

A phrase that used to mean *quiet devotion* has become a joke between us, the kind that only exists when love is sturdy enough to hold a little laughter.

That's the thing with Mormor. Her kindness doesn't wear bows. It doesn't coo or linger for applause. It's honest. It's raw. Sometimes, if you don't know her, her bluntness can feel a little sharp around the edges, like she's cutting through politeness just to get to the point. But for me, it's one of the reasons I love her. There's no guessing with Mormor. No passive-aggressive care or sentimental guilt-trips. Just action, truth, and the kind of loyalty that doesn't need a warm tone to be real.

And in a life where love so often came with conditions, hers has become one of the purest I've ever known.

Chapter 3

I don't remember much of the labour itself, except that Bella was there, holding my hand. I remember coming in and out of awareness, numb and mechanical. There was a midwife — kind, grounded, with the kind of voice that made you believe everything would turn out okay. That helped me stay inside my body just enough to give birth in it.

At one point, Bella leaned over, her eyes glassy and full, and said, "I see her head! She has so much hair!"

We both smiled, that exhausted, stunned kind of smile. The kind that says, *we made it*..

I didn't see Diana before Bella did. Bella cut the cord. She was the first to witness my daughter fully arrive into the world. We looked at each other, me with a human on my chest, her with tears still in her lashes, and it felt like our whole story — everything we survived, everything we loved through — had led to that moment. That look said: *We're still here. We made something that didn't break.*

That night, I was prescribed sleeping pills. My body was collapsing under the hormone crash, the pain, the emotional flood. And even then, I still couldn't sleep. Too wired, too weird, too euphoric, too everything. I remember fidgeting with the hospital bed remote like it was a video game controller, lifting myself up higher and higher until I was practically touching the ceiling. Bella looked over and caught me mid-levitation. "Are you high on childbirth?" she asked, laughing. W both burst out laughing.

She had Diana that night. Woke every two hours to feed her with a tiny syringe while I lay unconscious like a dairy cow on Xanax. When the nurses came in, they praised *my* feeding efforts, but it was Bella who'd been running the operation like a postpartum night shift supervisor. When we got home, she'd set alarms on her phone: *Diana Feeding.* Every three hours. When they rang, she'd quietly pick Diana up, walk her into the bedroom, and place her into my arms like something sacred. Then she'd step out, let me nurse, and repeat it all night long.

I would often say thank you, half-awake and blinking. She'd just shrug and whisper, "Of course. She's my baby girl."

That's what Diana is to Bella: *baby girl.* No godmother title. No best-friend-of-mom. No auntie. Just a presence too big for labels and too constant to question. I still don't know what to call her. She's not my partner. She's not a parent. Soulmate doesn't quite fit either... too corny, too Hallmark. But it's something like that. A person you orbit. The gravity you didn't know you needed until it held you through 3 a.m. feedings and 3 p.m. meltdowns.

Bella moved in with me. Not temporarily. Not as a guest. She just *did.* Four months. And I don't think I would've made it without her. Lisbeth and Michael also started taking Diana for one night every week. Just so I could sleep. Just so I could be a person again. That's how much I trusted them — and trust didn't come easy, not after what I came from. I couldn't even take a shower unless Diana was in my line of sight. So, for me to let them take her for the night... it meant everything.

I was hyper-attuned to every detail. The air quality, the background noise, the mood of whoever entered the room. I didn't expose Diana to alcohol. Or yelling. Or even strong perfume. I was terrified of pacifiers. What if she confused it with my nipple and forgot how to latch? I Googled that. I Googled everything. And then I Googled whether Googling too much could harm my baby. My brain never shut off. The midwife said it was normal. *Postpartum anxiety,* she called it. But it didn't feel normal. It felt like I was a one-woman surveillance team, obsessively scanning the world for threats my daughter couldn't yet name.

Still, I was doing it. We were doing it. And in all the madness, there were moments. Quiet ones. Turning points.

One night, Diana was finally asleep, and Bella and I were sitting in the kitchen. My hair was greasy, my body leaking from places I didn't want to think about, but Diana was safe, and so was I.

Bella looked over and said, "You're really doing it, you know?"

I didn't answer.

She added, "Like actually doing it. You're a mom."

And it hit me, somewhere between the third diaper and the second mental breakdown: oh shit, I'm the adult now.

PART 13

THE AUDACITY OF HEALING

Chapter 1

I wake up now with one thought: *I can't wait to see Diana today.* That's what stable feels like. Not the absence of pain, but the presence of purpose.

Back then, I'd wake up wondering: *How much more can I take? How do I end this without hurting anyone?*

Now I picture a boat. It still has holes. But I've stopped panicking. I fix them, one by one. And if the water rises too fast, I know where to go: Bella's boat, Lisbeth's, Michael's. I rest there. Gain strength. Then return to mine.

That's safety.

Therapy is grief disguised as conversation. I cry so hard some sessions I forget why I started. Then later, like puzzle pieces settling into place, I realize: *Oh. I named the bruise.* I made it visible. And suddenly, it didn't have a hold on me anymore. *I had a hold on it.*

I journal Diana's life in a notebook. Photos, notes, moments I know I'll forget someday. I write it so she can know me — really know me — the way I always wished I could've known my own mom. I hope one day she reads it and finds answers, not silence.

She already asks me to say sorry. "That wasn't kind,"

she'll say, and I apologize with my whole chest. Because she knows my sorry means something. That alone makes me know I'll never become the mother I had.

When Diana's sad, I kneel. I meet her eyes. I say, "Tell me." And she does. Even at three. Especially at three. When she breaks something, I say, "It's okay. We can clean it up together." I still flinch inside sometimes. My body remembers the bruises I got for broken plates.

But she won't.

Her cries used to terrify me. Not because they were loud, but because they were familiar. They woke something ancient in me. My nervous system still reacts, flinching like I'm back in a house where feelings were punishable.

But I've learned: her crying doesn't mean I'm failing.

It means she trusts me enough to feel.

So, I hold her. Breathe with her. I name it for her: Anger. Frustration. Sadness. Because once you name a feeling, you can tame it.

That's what trauma therapy teaches too: the body keeps the score, yes, but it also keeps the alarm. And sometimes the alarm won't know you're safe until you teach it. Until you respond to every false panic with: *I'm here. We're okay.*

Some days I fail. Some days I forget. Some days, I need to be reminded I'm not broken. I reach out. I ask for a hand on my back. A hug. A conversation about nothing. I just need to be seen, not looked at, *seen in*.

I try to treat myself the way I treat Diana, but sometimes it feels like pouring water into a wound. I grieve what I never had. It's unfair. And it's healing. All at once.

I've learned gentle parenting is not just for her. It's for me. It means saying, "You did your best today," even if my best looked messy. It means letting myself feel without punishment. Because when your trauma hijacks your internal compass, you start reacting to peace like it's war. And healing? Healing is learning to recalibrate, to trust calm.

Becoming a mother made me grieve mine all over again. But it also helped me forgive parts of her I hadn't yet. I see how hard parenting is. And I know she wasn't well. I wish she got help. I wish she dropped the dishes the night I told her I wanted to die. I wish she hugged me and said, "Start from the beginning." But she didn't. She chose denial. Because acknowledging my pain meant admitting hers.

I no longer wait for her to change. Some people don't. Because they won't. They've built entire personalities around being right. There's no space for truth in that.

But I changed.

I am the proof that people like me can.

Because someone; Bella, Lisbeth, Michael, saw me through eyes that didn't flinch. They stayed. And in that stillness, something in me healed. Slowly. Brutally. But it did.

And now I speak. In classrooms. At conferences. In rooms full of teenagers hiding bruises behind sarcasm and vapes. I tell them: *If you, or someone you know, is being abused, speaking up won't get you taken away. It might just get your family help. It might be the beginning of something better.*

And I say: *Don't do drugs* is the dumbest advice I ever got. Instead I tell them, *How badly do you want to become a slave?* Because that's what addiction is. Slavery with a smile.

To the teachers and social workers, I say: Don't just ask what's wrong with a child. Ask what's going wrong *around* them. A child's behaviour is a mirror. Look deeper. We need harbors, not checklists. Denmark needs professionals who can be present, not just efficient. If you're burnt out, please — step away. Vulnerable lives can't afford half-jobs.

My deepest grief is knowing I nearly didn't make it here. That I almost left this world without knowing who I'd become. I picture myself, scarf in hand, ready to

disappear. And I wish I could whisper:
You belong here. You are wanted. You are loved, by people you don't even know yet.
And I'd take the scarf and wrap it around her shoulders. Not to silence her, but to warm her. Then I'd tell her: *Hold on. Help is coming. You're going to be someone's safe place. You're going to be hers.*

I still struggle. With food. With flashbacks. I'm on meds for nightmares; can you believe there's a pill for that now?
My PTSD hasn't left me, it's just learned some manners. It still knocks before it barges in, most days. And when Diana cries, I still hear echoes, but now I breathe through them like a woman trying to hold in a sneeze during a funeral.
When Diana says, "I love you, Mom," and rolls her eyes because she knows I'm about to say it back again — *I love you, I'm proud of you, I protect you, I love you* — I say it anyway. Every night. Because she will never go to sleep not knowing.
She will never be her own alarm clock.
I am raising a child who can bite someone and then tell me. "I bit my friend today." And we talk. Because children don't act out for fun. Their prefrontal cortex isn't fully developed. They feel first. Think later. And it's my job to show her what accountability looks like, not punishment. She's allowed trial and error. She's allowed to learn. So am I.
Sometimes I look at her and cry. Not because she's sad, but because she's *safe*. I am parenting myself through parenting her. I apologize when I lose my patience. I say sorry like it matters, because it does.
And one day, I hope she says, "I'm glad you're my mom." If she never says it, I'll look at her joy. Her laughter. Her confidence. And I'll know.
We don't break our children when we've been broken

ourselves. We break the cycle. We become the emergency boat we never had.

I still believe in the bruises we can't see, not because they're invisible, but because we learned to make them that way; to tuck them behind jokes, behind survival. But if we dare to name them — gently, without apology — they start to loosen their grip.
That's how we take our power back.
The bruises we *can* see are different. They come later. They look like resilience. Like honesty. Like someone standing on a stage saying, *it almost killed me. But I lived.*
We are all just vessels. And some of us are very well-decorated wrecks. But if you listen — really listen — we will tell you what we've survived. Not in words. But in presence.
So, when you look at me now, don't be fooled by the calm. I am a storm that survived itself.
And the title?
The bruises we can't see aren't faint — they're erased, dismissed, repackaged as attitude or weakness. But once I stopped hiding mine, I saw what they were trying to teach me:
You stayed. You survived. You can begin again.
When we finally let our bruises be seen, they stop being secrets and start being signals. That's when the real healing begins, not when they fade, but when they're met with hands that say,
I see you.
You're safe now. They were maps etched beneath my skin, guiding me through the wreckage I once called home. For years, I patched it with silence, smiles, starvation... anything to avoid admitting I was drowning.
But the bruises knew.
The bruises never lied.
They pulsed like signal flares, not to shame me, but to guide me back to shore.

And I listened, finally.
Now that I've named them, I can carry them like medals, not because I won, but because I didn't vanish.
That I didn't jump overboard.
That I didn't sink quietly into the cold.
That I lived.
That I kept rowing, even when my arms shook and the sky stayed black for days.
That I held my daughter through the storm and said,
We're safe. I've got us. I'll learn to sail if I have to.
And when I couldn't, I didn't drown; I was lifted by Bella, Lisbeth and her daughters, my sisters Amanda and Mathilde, and Michael,
they pull me onto their deck,
saying, "Now rest". We'll anchor here until you can try again.
This is what healing became:
Not a perfect vessel gliding across calm waters,
but a boat repaired with gold where it once broke open.
The bruises we can't see didn't disappear. But they don't control the wheel anymore.
They shimmer now — sometimes, they scream — but mostly whisper: You're not her, look, you stayed.

And if the day ever comes where Diana is the one drifting, and she is tired, trembling, lost in a storm she can't name, I hope she remembers:
there is a light that never went out.
It's on my deck. And it's hers.

The rope doesn't need explaining.

She'll know where to tie it, not around her neck,
but to something that floats.
Because once, my mother told me to use a rope.
And I almost did.

But I chose to build a boat instead.
One that doesn't drag us under,
but keeps us breathing, together,
even when the storm doesn't pass.

See, Mom?
No ropes, just oars.

And a girl I'd cross oceans for,
who doesn't see the storm in me,
just the way I keep rowing toward her.
Because the rope didn't vanish.
I just gave it a new job:
keeping us tethered to the life I stayed for.

See, Mom?
You'll never get credit for the boat.
You did suggest the rope.
I chose where to tie it.

And that part is mine.

Acknowledgements

To Bella: you cut the cord, quite literally, and stayed through the unraveling and the re-weaving. You fed my baby, held my hand, and somehow managed to hold *me* too. You are whatever lives beyond friendship. There's no word for you, and maybe that's the point. Thank you for choosing me over and over again, even when I couldn't see myself clearly.

To Lisbeth (Ma) and Michael (Pa): you took me in when I barely recognized the girl in the mirror. You gave me a safe place, real food, boundaries that felt like love, and a garden where my nervous system could remember that calm exists. Thank you for becoming the kind of parents I didn't know I was allowed to have.

To Diana: you saved me without knowing it. You made me want to stay. You gave meaning to every scar I once hated. I hope you grow up knowing you were loved out loud, in full colour, every single day.

To every therapist who sat through my metaphors about boats and bruises and religious trauma while somehow managing not to fall asleep or call for backup: thank you. I mean it. I know I talk a lot.

And finally, to the reader: if you made it here, thank you for staying through the wreckage.

May your bruises shimmer too.

Author's Note

I didn't write this book to be inspirational. I wrote it because I didn't want to die with it still inside me.

It took years to gather the courage to tell the truth; not the polished one, but the raw, jagged, inconvenient version. The one where love and trauma live side by side. Where parenting is both a redemption arc and a minefield. Where addiction makes you laugh and then leaves you bleeding.

If you saw yourself in these pages, in the fear, the grief, the resilience, then you were never alone to begin with.

This book doesn't have a happy ending. It has a real one.

And that, to me, is everything.

— Luna Thomsen

Resources for Readers

If you or someone you know is struggling with...

Trauma / PTSD / Abuse

- **Børnetelefonen (DK): 116 111**
- **Headspace Danmark (free youth counseling): headspace.dk**
- **DIGNITY – Danish Institute Against Torture: dignity.dk**
- **International:**
    - **RAINN (USA): rainn.org**
    - **Befrienders Worldwide: befrienders.org**

Eating Disorders

- **Landsforeningen mod Spiseforstyrrelser og Selvskade (DK): lmsos.dk**
- **Mind UK: mind.org.uk**
- **NEDA (USA): nationaleatingdisorders.org**

Addiction

- TUBA Danmark: For children of substance-dependent parents
- Center for Rusmiddelbehandling: Find your local municipal support
- Narcotics Anonymous (Global): na.org

You deserve help, even if no one ever taught you to ask for it.

Discussion Questions for Book Clubs or Classrooms

1. What do "the bruises we can't see" mean to you personally?
2. Which moment in Luna's story hit you the hardest — and why?
3. What societal systems failed her — and where did people show up instead?
4. What role do chosen families play in breaking cycles of trauma?
5. What do we misunderstand about addiction and parenting?

Optional Activity:

Write a letter to your past self; the one who needed someone to say "You're not broken. You were never broken."

ABOUT THE AUTHOR

LUNA THOMSEN is a French-born writer, speaker, and mother living in Denmark. After surviving abuse in religious trauma, childhood abuse, addiction, and a brutal journey through the mental healthcare system, she now holds lectures on negative social control, vulnerability, healing, and conscious parenting.

She raises her daughter with gentleness, dark humor, and fierce intention, and still journals their lives together in a notebook filled with glue-stuck photos and honesty.

Follow her work at:
Instagram: @lunahopethomsen
Booking: (Danish, English):
lunahopethomsen@gmail.com

Connect With Luna Thomsen

Want to book Luna for a lecture, talk, or panel?
Reach out via:
Email: lunahopethomsen@gmail.com
Instagram: @lunahopethomsen

Speaking topics include:

- Parenting through trauma
- The psychology of invisible wounds
- Surviving negative social control
- Addiction and recovery in high-functioning survivors

Printed in Dunstable, United Kingdom

68392357R00139